LET THE LIGHT IN
UNITY FOR ALL

Author: Suzanne M. DeCarolis

MONSTRANCE: Permission of Saint Williams of York Catholic Church, Tewksbury, Mass.

FRONT COVER: ANDREW R. SOUTHWORTH

UNITY FOR ALL

UNITY FOR ALL

DEDICATED TO

THE ONE

UNITY FOR ALL

LET THE LIGHT IN

UNITY FOR ALL

ISBN: **978-1-7323587-0-6**

Printed in **USA**˙
Email: suzdecarolis@comcast.net

UNITY FOR ALL

UNITY FOR ALL

Thankful
FR. FRANCIS DEMERS, OMI

My confessor since 2010, who listens well and encourages
me to speak. I am Blessed because of your wisdom.

FR. PETER IMAJI, O.S.A.

Thank you for editing this book. Thank you for becoming my confessor #2,
Thank you for allowing me to lector for you

FR. ALBERT MACPHERSON, O.S.A.

Thank you for proof reading a chapter and taking the time out
of your busy schedule to help me.

Proof Readers
MARGARET MARY SINGLETON

For all your support in helping me with proof reading
this entire book. I am Blessed to have you as my friend.
Your patience and help was deeply appreciated.

LEO & ELENI CARAYANNOPOULOS

My co-workers who encourage me to speak at all times.
Eleni, a special thanks for proof reading a chapter as well.

MARK SEVERNS

Your help with a chapter and encouragement to trust in GOD

UNITY FOR ALL

UNITY FOR ALL

CONTENTS

UNITY FOR ALL

UNITY FOR ALL

The Journey

On August 6, 2009, my sister Jeanne DeCarolis passed away. It was very sad to see a young woman of only 54, who used to be so active in sports, so full of life, die such a horrible death of bone cancer! She always took such good care of herself. I continued to ask myself "why"? We had lost our father at the age of 67, to Leukemia, and now, my sister at the young age of 54! To make matters worse, my mother then became ill and she could not maintain her weight. She asked me to visit with her, and I did that as often as I could. Because of all the time I was spending with my mother, I did not have as much time to see my boyfriend, who I had been dating for 5 years. I was mourning my sister, and now trying to console my mother. I thought my boyfriend understood how emotionally exhausted I was, how stressed out I was, and how heartbroken I was, but I was wrong about him. Since I was too tired to see my boyfriend the next day, he decided to make plans with an ex-girlfriend who he had not seen in 35 years. I wasn't worried because he had often told me that 35 years ago, she had cheated on him and broken his heart. That evening, I called him and he did not call me back for four hours, which was making me very worried. Finally, at 11:30pm, I got the dreaded call. He told me he met with his ex-girlfriend that day, and he said they went out to dinner and then she invited him back to her place. To ease my worry, he told me nothing had happened, and they had just caught up on old times. He then asked me if I wanted to meet her and I said, "of course". The next day, I went to his house and my jaw dropped as he explained to me that he loved us both, wanted to marry us both and he was seriously considering becoming a Mormon. He took out his Mormon Bible to show me that a Mormon can have two wives. I was shocked over his bizarre behavior as he had always been a Catholic!

UNITY FOR ALL

Obviously, I was very upset, and I did not know what to do or how to react. This man was supposed to love me, to be my life partner. His ex-girlfriend had broken his heart, and now he wanted to marry her! I became sick with grief, shock and heartbreak. My mother and my son began to worry about what all this emotional stress was doing to my health. Thinking exercise would help clear my mind and ease my pain, I started to walk my dog a mile, two miles, and then six miles per day. As I walked, I tried to draw strength from my Catholic roots, and recited scriptures from the bible. Worried about me, my neighbor and friend suggested I go to the Eucharistic Adoration at St. Williams Church in Tewksbury. Mass. I decided to go, but when I got there, I did not understand the setting at the altar. I was told that Jesus was in the Eucharist. The Eucharist, I learned is where the Catholic Church consecrates the bread and the wine. The teaching is that the bread and the wine are the "host" and become, the body and blood of Christ. I went with my mother and we stayed for the hour. I felt drawn to the Eucharist and started to go to Adoration every day. I found going to Adoration very comforting and peaceful. I began to feel more and more drawn to this sacred Eucharist. After years without really following religion, I started praying and bought myself the Catholic bible to read while I was in there. I was beginning to feel better, but each time I left Adoration I cried in my van in the parking lot. I met a very nice woman one day when she thought it was her turn to spend an hour with Jesus.

As it turned out, she had the days mixed up. I told her my story and I broke down and cried. I told her how hurt I was, and what was happening with my boyfriend. She said if my boyfriend loved me as much as I loved him, he would not let me suffer like this. She was right, because it was then I realized he indeed had a cold heart even after our five year relationship. I was hurting so much because I had lost him to this other woman, worse yet one who had already broken his heart once. I knew I loved him more than she ever could, and I was so torn up inside over the betrayal of trust. The woman I met at Adoration told me to read about Tobit

UNITY FOR ALL

in the Bible and read a scripture on St. Raphael. I read both stories, and began to gain some more understanding. The woman then told me that in order to heal, to get over my pain and the betrayal, that I had to give my boyfriend to Jesus. She was very clear about this, and I knew that I could not do it. I could not stop crying over the fact that I had to offer him to Jesus. I did not want to lose him, I loved him so much. I wanted to share my life with him, forever. How could I just let him go? She said, "Ask Jesus to take the pain from you so that you do not have to suffer anymore". I cried so much I was embarrassed with myself over the incident. She asked me if I had Rosary Beads and I let her know I had my grandmothers and grandfathers.

My grandmother gave me those beads a few weeks before she passed away, in 2002, and told me her husband prayed three times a day using the Rosary. I never knew any of the prayers for the beads and put them in my dining room hutch. She had to leave, so I stayed behind at Adoration, lost and confused. It took me a good long time to come to terms with the fact that I had to let him go. He was already gone to me anyway. He had betrayed me, he wanted a life with this other woman and there was nothing else I could do. I had lost him and holding on to the pain was destroying me. It took everything in me, but in a moment of raw faith, I finally asked Jesus to take him from me.

Right after I did this, as I left Adoration, instead of getting into my van and crying, I walked out to my van and left with a smile on my face. I did not know or understand at that point what was happening to me. I just knew I felt better. A wave of relief came over me, a release of pain if you will. It all happened so fast, and yet I felt the result immediately. I felt as if God had laid his hands upon my shoulders and told me "everything will be ok." I drove home and took those beads out of my dining room hutch, and went online to look for the prayers for the Rosary Beads. I began my first prayer with those beads on the couch. The next morning I awoke to a feeling of peace. It is very hard to put into words because the emotions were so fresh, so strong. Everything around

UNITY FOR ALL

me felt peaceful, and as it should be. I no longer felt the lump in my chest, the heartbreak, the fear, the betrayal, the anger, the grief. It felt like the elephant that was sitting on my chest was suddenly gone. My pain was gone. My heartache, it had left my body and my mind. The best way I can think to describe it is that I felt alive, and so full. I felt so wonderful, all over, like every little detail around me was sparkling. If you have ever had the feeling of everlasting love come over you, then you know what I mean. I felt so loved and protected. I knew that my soul, my spirit, my heart were deserving of love, not pain and grief. I knew I had been healed. Healed of all the negative things that had been happening to me and around me.

I felt warm inside, like a warm glow of white light was flowing through me, and it was everywhere. Instead of feeling empty inside, I felt so full of light and love. It was like this huge void in my life had been filled up. I loved myself, and Jesus taught me that. I was in love with the feeling of being in Love. I felt so good, I immediately answered my mom's email and told her how good I felt and that I was going to Adoration. When she received my email, she thought I was kidding with her. I then went to see her and she could tell by my face that I had a glow! I told her I felt wonderful and how I met this woman at Adoration and how I read the story on Tobit, and read the scripture on St. Raphael and felt wonderful. This feeling of LOVE took over my life. I was at peace. I felt the most inner beauty and peace that I have ever felt in my life. I was in Love with Love. I felt like a new woman, and this new woman wasn't going to sit in the van and cry anymore. This new woman had a mission, to share her experience with everyone and anyone who would listen. I knew my days of pain and grieving were over. In a word, I felt blessed. I finally understood that "God dwells in our midst, in the Blessed Sacrament of the altar." – **St. Maximilian Kolbe**.

This feeling lasted for about 3 weeks. I then started to feel sad and was told by the same woman to go back to the altar and ask Jesus to help. I did just that and by the next morning I had the most inner peace ever! It was Thanksgiving day, and my brother was cooking for the family at his house and my family could sense my inner peace, and my glow. My mother and my brother thought I was a completely different person. I felt completely at peace and had the most beautiful feeling of my life. I still have this feeling, and it continues to get stronger each day.

The more time I spend at Adoration, or just attending a scheduled Mass, the more Blessed I feel. Jesus has changed my life completely. I am closer to Jesus, I pray often, I can't stop talking about my blessings. I share it with others, I encourage people to pray to your rosary as well as spend time with the Blessed Sacrament at an Adoration.

I realize now that everything in life happens for a reason. I needed to find myself and I did through Jesus. I believe the Eucharist at Adoration saved my soul. It has enriched my life and taught me to love myself. I now put God first in my life. He has changed my life and I would not trade this feeling for anything in the world.

Just an hour with Jesus…. "Let the Light In" and may Jesus give you the same inner peace and love he's given me.

God Bless.

Suzanne

Chapter One

I did not realize at the time what was happening to me except that I felt different. I felt like a different being was filling my soul with an inner peace and joy that I have never experienced before my conversion. I knew when this would occur, and I just went with it since it was completely out of my control. This feeling of total peace was consuming me.

I remember bringing my son to school daily with the feeling of Joy in knowing I was going to spend the day with Jesus. I would hurry myself down to the chapel after Mass at Saint Williams church in Tewksbury, Ma. As I opened the door a feeling of compassion and trust began immediately. I knew I belonged with Him and I walked up to the altar and it was there we looked at each other. As I glanced at Him I knew I had found my special place and I felt the need to stay until I had to pick up my son at school at 2:00 pm. I would kneel at the alter for about 15 – 20 minutes before sitting down. There I noticed images in the Eucharist and hearing whispers of words but could not quite put them together. As I said, the Lord was preparing me, and I was on a new Journey I did not know anything about. When I was in my chair I felt an inner peace come over me from the top of my head down to my toes. It was so beautiful and I was told by a friend nearby to recite prayers fast and consistent. I felt upon doing this the Holy Spirit would continue, and I could get a longer sense of a beautiful experience. This started to happen daily as I started praying more consistent. I felt him inside my soul and that inner peace was so beautiful I longed for Him daily. I noticed each time I left and walked up the stairs my legs felt lifeless and my body felt as if it did not even exist. There was a sense of peace that stayed with me when I walked out that door to head to my vehicle.

I felt as if He was coming home with me and all I had to do was spend time with Him daily to enjoy this profound sense of peace which was consuming my whole being. This went on for days to weeks to months. I was falling in love with Jesus!!!

One day while praying at home I went into a deep meditation and upon opening my eyes I heard a whisper and saw a white light. As I came closer to this white light I heard the words, (in a man's voice), "Father", "Son", "Holy Spirit", and the white light vanished. It went out like a light – and I awoke immediately. I did not know why Jesus wanted me to experience that. There was no fear but I do not know what he was trying to show me.

I started reciting the rosary and again went into another deep meditation and heard a man's whisper. Although I did not understand the language this deep peace again came over me and I continued praying because I longed for this deep union of peace. How magnificent I thought this is and all I have to do is pray non-stop to feel this beautiful experience.

As the days continued I kept going to church for the Homily and Eucharist and heading to Adoration right afterwards. I longed to be with Him daily. I would then pick up my son at school. Andrew was in 11th grade and had a job after work which I had to bring him. I then went back to Adoration until it was time to pick him up and spent another five hours there in deep meditation. I longed for Jesus morning and evening because I knew my soul could achieve greater peace being in His presence. My mother would often meet me there as well.

A few days later I met my good friend Geri at Adoration and we decided to go out to breakfast. I told her some of the things which was happening to me in Adoration. She suggested I go back and tell Jesus "YES".

I realized I left my red hat in the Chapel and needed to go back anyway and pick it up. When I walked in the door I found my hat was on the chair. I picked it up and went to the altar to tell Jesus, "YES". When I turned around a woman introduced herself as "Barbara". She told me it was not her day to be there, but Saint Joseph told her to cover the hour and she was to meet someone who needed Holy Salt. I was surprised as I never even heard of Holy Salt. We started talking and she told me the importance of having Holy Salt in your house and for our souls. I followed her out to her car and she gave me a bottle of Holy Salt.

UNITY FOR ALL

She told me I needed to cleanse my soul. This meant I needed to pour it in Holy Water and put it in a Spray Bottle and spray myself while reciting some words. I was a little scared and wondered why I needed to do this but I agreed. I rushed to the store and purchased a pink Spray Bottle about 7" high and I went to the Lowell Shrine on Lee Street, Lowell, Ma, and filled it with Holy Water. I then poured all of the Holy Salt into this bottle. The next morning, I had to spray my body with it after my shower and recite "In the Name of Jesus", "I Cleanse my Body and Soul". I did this consistently for 30 days. On the last day when I sprayed myself the clear water now came out RED! I took it to my Spiritual Director, Father David, and he thought it happened because the bottle was pink. He suggested I find a clear bottle and do it again. I never did it again and threw it away afterwards.

I continued going to morning Mass since I was not working at the time. I was looking for a job and could not get pass the interview. It was simple I would bring my son to school and go to Mass at Saint Williams in Tewksbury, and then spend the day with Jesus. I was very happy with this routine which was happening every single day for five days a week and Mass on the weekends.

One day, while sitting in Adoration in Tewksbury I heard a man's whisper, **"WORD".** I thought to myself, "What does this mean"? I do not know what to do with WORD. I asked a friend sitting near me and she suggested I buy a Bible. I signed up for Bible Study at Saint Williams and started to read the bible. I admit I never owned a Bible although my parents had a Bible and both were very religious. I was not as religious and was in infancy stages similar to one starting or beginning something new. I had to learn from scratch and the only way to know the Bible is to Read the Bible.

John 1:14: And the WORD became Flesh and made his dwelling among us, and we saw his glory the glory as of the Fathers son, Full of Grace and Truth! (usccb.org)

It was after that I decided to spend all night in Adoration. I wanted to see if I would enjoy it and if I felt any different during the all night vigil. It was Christmas Eve and I wanted to be there for His coming. I enjoyed this time very much and realized into the morning hours it is even more peaceful and still. There is a deeper peace in the middle of the morning hours or late into the evening. Saint Williams has Perpetual Adoration and there is always someone there. At Saint Williams we all choose an hour to be with Jesus. We keep a cross which we transfer to one soul after another depending on who has the next hour. Jesus is never alone in our Chapel. I stayed all night and wide awake. I left at about 6:00 am, and never felt tired. When I came home I had to clean house, put a turkey in the oven and get ready for my family at noon time. I never felt better and was very wide awake.

A few months passed and while sitting in Adoration I heard a woman's whisper, "Let The Light In". I thought to myself, "What a beautiful message but what does it mean"? I met my friend Steve Southard, that morning and I began to tell him in Mass that I heard a woman's whisper" and she said, "Let The Light In". Shortly after that, the Mass started and the Homily of the day was, "Let the Light in your LIFE". Steve looked at me and laughed and I did not know what to think. I was told Jesus was preparing me for many gifts and to share them with others. Let the Light in your heart is most powerful, that is where the entire life takes its spiritual strength and nourishment.

John 8:12, Jesus spoke to them again saying, "I am the Light of the world. Whoever follows me will not walk in darkness, but will have the Light of Life". (usccb).

UNITY FOR ALL

Chapter Two

I heard that Saint Williams was having a Healing Mass and I had never gone to one. I really wanted to go and experience this Healing Mass. The priest belongs to an order known as the Oblates of Mary Immaculate. His name is Father McAlear, and he has travelled the whole world and offers a healing Mass during which he brings out the Eucharist and has prayers and healing services with oil that he blessed. I heard very good stories about this priest. I went to Mass that morning and attended one of his events. We were told to stand at the altar and have our hands in front of us open to receive his blessings. He approached each person and looked into your eyes with a message from Jesus. When he came to me I remembered asking him to help me with my "stutter" and he said, **"You have peace"**. I nodded and said," **"Yes, I have Peace"**. He blessed me on the forehead and gazed into my eyes. I felt as if Jesus was looking right at me. I felt another peace come over me and a strange feeling on the right side of my face, it's as if something had left that area. I could see in a wider angle. I had no idea what it was before, and all I knew was that I had a better view than before because something was lifted. I went downstairs to the Chapel which was this time in the large lower church. They had the Eucharist on the alter. I sat there with my friend Geri. I fell into a deep deep peace right in my chair. I was slain in the spirit and Geri had to leave and could not wake me so she left. I came out of it about 45 minutes later. I remembered everything that I saw while in this beautiful state of peace. I was in another place unknown to me. I was walking with another man much older than I. He was wearing all white with a cap on his head. While walking I noticed lots of pillars and marble floors.

It was a long walk and when we got to the window looking down I saw thousands of people. Most of the people had on yellow hats and the man I was with kept repeating "NEW WORLD NEW WORLD". It was so amazing.

As the days continued, I kept visiting Jesus each morning in the Chapel at Saint Williams in Tewksbury. I started telling more friends about what was happening to me and more and more started meeting me there. Each time I would arrive with a smile letting Jesus know I was inviting more souls to witness such a beautiful experience. I thought "Why should I keep this to myself?", and if he helped me in so many ways I should help Him by inviting others. Everyone agreed to come and soon I realized all of us are seeking the same peace for our Souls.

One day while sitting in Adoration in this deep deep peace I felt this very strong presence. I never felt it this strong before, and definitely not like this. I then heard the words and this time not in a whisper as in the past. I heard a man's stern voice say "**LIVE YOUR LIFE**"!!! I thought about it and wrote it down. I asked my priest about it and he felt I was spending too much time in Adoration. I then went back to Adoration and told Jesus I can never experience the same feelings in the world as I can in Adoration. There would be no possible way. I wanted to spend all my free time in Adoration. It was exactly a month later while sitting in Adoration I heard, again in a loud strong voice, "**I FORGIVE YOU**". I did not understand this and asked "What did I do to be forgiven?". How selfish I thought to myself. All the things in my life that I did wrong and never listened. He now Forgave me??? I had to let the priest know He said these things and I made an appointment with Father John Hanley, who was our Pastor at that time.

Since my conversion in 2009, I only heard this loud voice two times and these two phases. Everything else was spoken in a woman's or man's whisper. I knew without a doubt He was trying to tell me many things and all I had to do was listen and pray consistently.

I continued my Journey with the lord by attending morning Mass and then Adoration. Later I would pick up my son from school where he was a senior and take him to work. I wish I had a job too and began praying for a job. It was difficult finding one and I knew I needed to work.

One morning I woke up after my alarm went off and I heard the words "JESUS, "JESUS", "JESUS". This kept being said in my head over and over again. I tried to not listen because this was coming from my conscience and not a whisper. I did not know why I was repeating this. I decided to rush to Mass and listen to the Homily. Even on my drive to Saint Williams I heard it over and over again. As I sat down and listened to the Homily, the message was to Follow Jesus. To give away all your possessions and follow him. I thought to myself, "Where am I to go? "My son was a senior in High School and on his way to college". I apologized to Jesus and said, not this time. I am not going to follow you. I went to Adoration afterwards and began to feel his presence come over me. I needed to tell Him I can not follow Him. As I said this I felt a great peace. I have too many issues. I am not a good public speaker and I stutter. I am not in a position in my life to drop everything and follow you. Please forgive me.

One day while in Adoration at Saint Williams, this great peace came over me this time very strong. I told Jesus I can't follow him, I stutter. Besides, how can I speak for him in a larger group when I purposely did not go to college for fear of public speaking. Jesus said to me, "**YOU CAN SPEAK**". I did not know what to say. I was speechless! He acknowledged too that He was correct. I can speak and one on one I speak very well. I knew what He was asking me to do and I find it impossible to even think about it.

I continued to visit the Chapel and invite my friends. One by one everyone came and all said the same story, they felt the immediate peace upon leaving. I invited my best friend since 6th grade, Roseann Karlberg, who is no longer Catholic and is a Born Again. She said Jesus gave her a peace she never experienced in her life. My son agreed to go and my sister. My mom joined me and also came often on her own. She had digestive problems at night and would visit at night and told me she would always go and pray and within thirty minutes go home and go to bed and sleep all night. Jesus was healing all of us with all kinds of issues.

No souls are alike and all of us are suffering with something different, I thought to myself. I also thought this would be the best way I could help Jesus. I could invite all souls not just friends. I knew deep in my soul this was making Jesus very happy. The more souls I brought to Him the deeper peace He left in my soul and also the greatest Joy. That Joy was contagious too. There is a tremendous Joy in doing the lord's work. It starts with one soul at a time.

The Lord had me working double time. I found myself in places telling others about Adoration. They never heard of Adoration and because they lived in town or next to my town, I felt the urge to tell them about Adoration.

They went and felt immediate peace. Some said they would go and I do not know if they went or not and others met me there. This was becoming a part time job. I felt the need to share with as many people who would listen. I realized Jesus was doing this as he sent me places where people would talk about problems in their own life and I would initiate the conversation about Adoration and they agreed to go. I did not ever meet these souls prior. I just felt an urgency to get this message out to everyone I met. I felt so delighted in doing this for Jesus! I knew when we arrived my soul was filled with such a happy and excited feeling each and every visit. This lasted the whole time I was there and His presence as soon as I prayed, Father, Son and Holy Spirit came upon us.

I began to see souls in the Eucharist and not knowing who they were. I remember telling Geri I saw a child sitting in a chair. Geri did not know what to make of it and I began to tell her what I saw. I saw a child sitting in a chair and this child was holding a stick in one hand. He wore a straw hat, red jacket and blue outfit. I kept starring at the Eucharist and I was at the altar trying to figure it all out. Why did Jesus want me to see this image and who was this soul, I thought to myself. The following week I went to a store and the same image in the Eucharist was for sale on a shelf.

I bought it and took it home and asked Geri. She said God has given you a gift and this is Saint Nino De Atocha, a Spanish version of Jesus. I was happy to have this in my possession, however I still did not know why Jesus wanted me to see him in the Eucharist. Little did I know that this was the beginning of more to come in the future.

On another day I am at the altar and I see a man on the left side of the Eucharist. He comes up very clear. I could almost pick out all his facial features perfectly. I saw a man with white hair, and it is parted on one side. He is wearing a black jacket, white collar. He appeared for three weeks on the left hand side of the Eucharist. I had no idea who was this soul, but prayed for him during my whole time in Adoration. I would pray for his soul and asked the lord to keep him well. I devoted my rosary for his soul. I did not know if he had passed or if he was a living soul.

I started seeing Jesus from ten feet from the altar. He would appear to me each and every time. I also saw the Blessed Mother's face as well. I kept my eyes focused on the Eucharist. During the first hour I would see Jesus and the second hour I would see Mary. I had shared this experience with others in the Chapel who had seen the same as me on other occasions. This brought on a deeper meaning and I was told it was meant for me during my hour to experience their love for us.

It was in May and I finally landed an interview and was excited about working again. The position was part time about twenty hours a week. I decided I should go for it and work my way into full time. It was an inside sales position with an office supply company. I was greeted by a black lab who looked just like my black lab. My dog was a male and his was a female. His dog was very friendly. While in his office I noticed these beautiful watercolor paintings. My mother was a watercolor artist as well, which is what I told him. His mom had won many ribbons and did portraits. I have never seen art as well done as hers in my life! I was so impressed with her paintings. He had a picture of himself with his tennis team and said he almost made it to the finals. I told him I had a tennis court in my back yard. I even invited him for a game sometime as we chuckled about it. Then I met David his business partner. David ran the operations part of the business. They showed me my new office which was tiny and quaint. I told them I stutter sometimes, and they told me they could not detect it at all.

I was so happy to be working again and I wanted to share the news with my friends at Adoration. I was going to visit Jesus at night in the Chapel. I remember getting there and kneeling at the altar. I saw three children staring at me. I had no idea who these souls were. I noticed two girls and one boy. I could also describe them perfectly. When I went to my seat they were in the Eucharist staring at me. No matter where I sat in the Adoration room there they were in the Eucharist. My friend, Joan, a 3rd order Carmelite for over 25 years had called me and I told her I saw two girls and one boy staring at me in the Eucharist and they are all standing up! She told me today is **May 13th,** our Feast day of Lady Fatima. I never heard of that before, and she told me they probably want you to pray to the intercession of Saint Francisco. I decided at that point to do as she suggested and read about them.

In June 2010, while in my office and making phone calls, David came in. He sits down and I felt a little uncomfortable knowing he wanted to listen to me make phone calls. I started stuttering talking to him and he immediately started mocking me. He wouldn't stop and began to do it every time he felt like teasing me. I again asked him to stop and he did. The next day he did it again and again and again. I decided to bring this up to several of my friends at church. They told me to take it to the altar. Give it to Jesus the same way I gave my ex-boyfriend to Jesus. I found out he was gay and thought if he is going to pick on my stuttering I will pick on his lifestyle.

As the days progressed the more he picked on me the more I picked on him. I even thought of resigning because I felt my stuttering would definitely get worse if this was to continue on a daily basis.

UNITY FOR ALL

I went to church and begged Jesus to help me. I remember it was August and David went on vacation. I was told I had to work non stop in getting appointments for my boss and also help with deliveries while David was on vacation in Maine.

Then I received the dreaded news. David was very sick. While he was in Maine he came down with MRSA. It was on his back and spreading quite rapidly. He was in the hospital in Maine and since they could not help him they sent him to Boston. He texted me and asked me to pray for him. I was a little surprised at this because I was not allowed to talk about Adoration at work and now, after all this time of him picking on me, he wanted my prayers. I agreed I would pray for him if he promised he would never ever pick on my stuttering again and come with me to Adoration. I don't know why I wanted him to come to Adoration, maybe since he was protestant and has not been to church in a long time I thought it would be interesting to hear his thoughts about our Blessed Chapel. He agreed. I found out a few days later David had a full recovery! He even came back to work about a week later. He showed us the big patch he had on his back which now was a little hole and had a bandage.

Our co-worker Rita had changed his bandage for him while he was at the office. He told me he felt great and was going to join me in Adoration as soon as he had the time. David did come back to work eventually and did come to Adoration at Saint Williams in Tewksbury. I even told my Pastor at the time he was coming to Adoration and mentioned he is Protestant. I met him in the parking lot of Saint Williams in Tewksbury.

We walked downstairs together and sat down. I explained to him we would go to the altar and he can thank Jesus. I put my grandmother's rosary in my hand and we walked to the altar. I thanked Jesus over and over again for healing David and also I asked Jesus to let him be who he was "Born to Be".

We then sat down in our chairs and I let him hold my grandmother's rosary for the remaining 45 min. David was very relaxed and at peace and told me he understood my desire to be there. He came again and again. I saw him there a few times while walking into the Chapel. He came alone. I was happy he found a place where he could go and speak to Jesus. I knew also at that point we would become good friends and put all our differences behind us. We attended a healing Mass with Father Whalen once and we did the rosary there. I knew Jesus wanted me to love him as my brother and not to judge him. I loved David from that point on and knew he was a good friend for me and I could always trust him in life.

A few weeks went by and I was visiting with my mom in her townhouse in Tewksbury. I was telling her about David and how Jesus healed him. She was surprised he even went to Adoration because he is protestant. I told her it was a beautiful testimony to Faith and Love of Jesus. It was about 5:30 PM and my cell phone rang. It was David and he wanted to know if I would meet him and Angelo at Adoration. He told me Angelo was an ex-boyfriend who had received some bad news from his doctor and needed Adoration. I told my mom I had to leave at that very instant. I was meeting David at Adoration and his friend. My mother was shocked and said, "How can this be"? I told her I must trust Jesus with everything. I left her house and went immediately to Saint Williams in Tewksbury.

I met David and Angelo and the three of us went to the Chapel downstairs. I had his friend sitting on one side of me and David on the other. There we were in Adoration. I could not wait to introduce him to Jesus. We went to the altar and then sat down. His friend was very anxious and nervous at the same time. I told him I would call upon the Holy Spirit and for him to just let Jesus take over. Let him heal you as surrendering is the first step in this process. He felt the presence and the peace. He was out of it for about thirty minutes and when he came awake he told me he felt better. He told me he would let me know in a few days if everything turned out well. A few days later I heard David on the phone with him and everything turned out fine. He had a healing and he was fine. He also was very grateful and I told him since he is Catholic to come back. Come Back and sit with our Lord.

UNITY FOR ALL

I believed now Jesus was healing everyone who walked in the Chapel and was definitely the Peace Maker. This is what Jesus wanted of me. I was doing all he asked of me if it was soul by soul and I would be obedient to helping souls as much as I could. Besides, I felt the presence as well and the Joy was consuming my soul. I've made many new friends in this process. I understood more of what the role of a priest was because souls felt the need to tell me everything and I did not have the background to help them. All I could offer was an ear and advice to seek a priest. Most of them did not want to seek a priest and some did go back to Confession and then to church. I knew in order for them to receive Communion after being away from church more than a year to fifty five years, they had to go to Confession first, and then have penance from the priest prior to receiving Jesus in Communion. Many of them met me at Saint Joseph's Shrine in Lowell, Ma. I invited them to Confession, to the store downstairs, and to the noon Mass in the upper church.

As I said, it was all for Jesus. I knew this is what he wanted and I was doing His service.

Adoration was my coming back to God and it was their coming back to him as well. I had a feeling of Love, Trust and Faith and he was number one in my life. I wanted to do all He asked of me and this was the best I could offer with the time I had now. If you only knew the feeling I felt inside my soul each time one soul was meeting me for Adoration. I had this presence come upon me and it is a strong presence and a Joy that only comes from loving Him, knowing Him and trusting Him in all things.

I soon knew in my heart to invite Deborah and Paula to Adoration. I have not seen them for a few years and wanted them to meet Jesus in Adoration. Paula was a hair stylist and a gourmet cook. She invited me for dinner and asked me if I needed a haircut which I did. I prayed before the Blessed Sacrament for them as well. They both came to Adoration.

UNITY FOR ALL

Deborah and Paula said it was peaceful. Deborah came back a few times seeking His peace which she received at each visit. They joined me at a healing Mass with Father Albert MacPherson, OSA, in Methuen.

Deborah invited me to her mother's house in Revere. I never met her mom who at the time had early stages of Dementia. Marie was very nice and greeted us at the door. I walked into this cute little ranch and sat in the kitchen. I brought Holy water for Marie since her back was very sore. She complained of this pain on and off the whole time I was present. We prayed a rosary and spoke of Jesus. A call came in and I went into the living room where Jerry was sitting down.

Jerry has been married to Marie for about twenty five years, her second husband. He told me he has cancer and had just three months left to live. He also told me he was Jewish and did not believe in God. I asked him if I could bless his forehead with Holy Oil and let's leave the healing up to GOD. I saw him many months later and he did go into remission. I went to a 4th of July party at Deborah's house and he was there. Deborah said, remember "Sue" she prayed over you – and you survived! I told him "Remember, I told you GOD is the Healer and you have work to do here it was not your time". I believe I was sent to Marie's house to bring Faith to Jerry.

(Jerry lived till 2015. I will always remember that the one with No Faith is the One who needs the prayers the most. We must all pray for those who have No Faith.)

My days were consumed with work daily and then walking the dog and picking up my son at school and taking him to work and then finding time for Jesus in my most sacred place, Adoration. I was keeping my weekends open for meeting people at the Chapel and introducing them to Jesus. This was what I believed he wanted me to do and I was completely open to helping him. Each soul had a different story to tell about how much their life had changed in just one visit.

UNITY FOR ALL

My friend Joan O'Neil invited me to a Carmelite meeting. She asked me to join her group and I thought I would like to go and see what it was all about before committing. I also asked if I could bring Geraldine, my good friend. Geri came as well the first time and immediately had an interest in joining. I felt called to be with Jesus only in Adoration. I did not join but I attended as a guest.

One thing I did notice was they passed around some brochures at my first visit and I recognized the face on the trifold. I could not believe my eyes! The man who was staring at me in the Eucharist, on the left hand side for three weeks was "**Brother Andre Bessette**". He was going to be canonized a Saint. I didn't know why the Lord wanted me to see him before he was canonized a Saint. I mentioned my excitement to Joan and Geri. It was interesting to read that he passed away on January 6th, which happens to be my father's birthday! All these things are turning out to be God "Coincidences

I began talking to Kevin McQuaid a friend from my childhood. He had dated my sister when she was about sixteen. They had broke up and gone separate ways. It had been close to thirty years since I spoke with him last. He married and lived in Western Massachusetts. His wife Kay had passed away two years prior to us speaking and his son passed away three years as well. He was very depressed as anyone would be after losing two people you love very much. I knew his mother, Helena McQuaid as she was still counting money for Saint Williams of Tewksbury for twenty plus years.

He told me briefly about a pain in his collar bone which he had for over 26 years. He had many operations on this collar bone and nothing worked. He was in pain most days with no relief whatsoever. I told him about the Ministry and my love for Jesus. I mentioned I would like to pray for him. He said it would take a miracle to help him. I said, "If Jesus can heal you will you come to Saint Williams in Tewksbury, and thank him?" and, "Will you come to Mass and Adoration?". A week later and I received the phone call. Kevin said all the pain has left him and he felt he had a healing. He was coming to Tewksbury for Christmas. He said his mother was so happy to hear the news and he was also coming to thank Jesus in person.

It was Christmas Eve and he met me at Saint Williams in Tewksbury. They had moved the Adoration Chapel to the rectory. I met him at the rectory and we went in. He sat there and prayed. I was so happy and very much appreciated that Jesus helped him. It was such a touching moment to witness Kevin at church after forty years and he sat in the front row staring at Jesus and praying. I was happy for Jesus and happy for Kevin. My friend Josephine O'Connor walked in and I introduced her to Kevin. She said she had been praying for him for three years. She was happy to see him in Adoration and we thought what a miracle this is indeed! Kevin also came to the midnight Mass and sat in the front pew. After Mass we went to my house where I made italian wedding soup and we talked till 3:00 A.M.

I started spending most of my weekends meeting people that I met at Adoration at Saint Williams in Tewksbury. I never kept in contact with them afterwards. I either met them at the prayer groups or shopping at different places, and some even at the doctor's offices. I found myself evangelizing on a daily basis. I also was reciting my rosary everywhere and every second of the day that I had free thought. My whole life became a life with Jesus. I spoke with Jesus every day and felt this strong desire to bring souls to Him and only Him. He was whom I trusted and I loved deeply. I still had the fear of public speaking and knew deep down what He really wanted me to do. Yet, I loved to talk about Him to others and this I knew was my desire of all things.

I was appreciative of when he entered my soul and gave me this everlasting peace. It's as if I could feel a warm light surrounding me and this feeling of peace which was consuming me. I felt a passion like I never felt in my life and how can I even explain this to my friends as they saw me light up with even a mention of the name "GOD".

UNITY FOR ALL

I was in love with GOD. I wanted to be with Him all the time and it happened so deeply in His presence at my secret place in the Chapel in Tewksbury, at Saint Williams.

One day at work my boss came into my office when he was leaving and as he walked out the door he glanced back at me and I saw the "devil" in his eye. I was scared out of my wits. I only saw this once before in another soul. I did not know what to do or what it meant. I needed to tell someone and she told me to have a Mass in his name. During this time his brother had passed away. I decided I would have a Mass for him and his brother. I proceeded to the church and they told me I had to book both of these Masses three months into the future, because they did not have a time slot available. I set up two different Masses in each of their names.

It was now 2011, and I was sitting in Adoration at the rectory since our chapel had a flood. I remember sitting in Adoration before the Blessed Sacrament. I asked Jesus, "How do I explain this beautiful place". I heard a woman's whisper, **"UNITY FOR ALL"**. I thought to myself, "What is Unity for All?". I had no idea what this meant. The same time sitting there I noticed Father Croft was sitting a few rows up from me and I could ask him. He stood up and was walking towards me and I asked him. He said something, but it was too much for me to understand. I asked him to make it simple. He said, "GOD always wanted ONE Church". I could understand that much better. I started to think, "One Church", "One God". Lord, lead me and I will bring the souls to you, Jesus! It came to me that I needed to bring all souls to Jesus. Not just Catholic Souls – all Souls of all Religions. If Roseann is Born Again and she continued to join me in Adoration, why couldn't I invite others to come as well.

I told Jesus I would do it and all he had to do was put the souls before me and I would tell them about this beautiful place which brings Love, Peace and Joy. I will speak to souls one – on – one which is what I was already doing. I went back to the altar and said, "Yes".

In March of 2011, while sitting in Adoration I heard "On the 13th day It will be in the Eucharist". I sat there not knowing what this meant. Again, I thought, I will wait until March 13th and just be patient. On the 13th, my friend Ray Turcotte came to see me in the parking lot. He had a picture that was in the Chapel and he wanted me to bring it home because they were working on the walls in the Chapel. I looked at this picture which happened to be of the Eucharist and Jesus was in the middle! What a confirmation! I took it home and hung it proudly on my fireplace. I was simply amazed at how accurate Jesus had become in preparing me to listen to His word. I also realized it was Lent and during Lent anything can happen!

I remember in March while sitting at home in my family room I began to pray a rosary. I started asking Jesus, should I move or should I stay. My father had built me this beautiful home back in 1988. I loved the house but it was breaking down all around me. I had a part time job and I could not keep up with the demands of a large home. After I finished my rosary I got up and I heard in a woman's whisper, "**F**orget **T**he **P**ast **M**ake **N**ew **M**emories". I was very much surprised and turned around and looked right at the picture on the fireplace! I could not believe it. I called my Spiritual Director, Father Demers, and asked to see him at once. When I went to visit with him he assured me that it was time to sell the house and move forward.

I went to Adoration shortly afterwards and to my surprise I get up to the altar and see numbers. This was the first time I saw numbers in the Eucharist. I saw **0512**. I knelt and stayed and stared. I thought to myself, why is He showing me **0 5 1 2**. This must be a mistake. As I knelt there 5 minutes, 10 minutes, 15 minutes, **0 5 1 2**. I then went back to my seat. I still saw these numbers from 10 feet away. I told many people about this and was told to wait and be patient. My friend Kevin told me his birthday is May 12th.

UNITY FOR ALL

One day in March I was in my chair praying the rosary at my house in Tewksbury. Within fifteen minutes I heard a terrible scream of a devil. It was so dreadful and scary I jumped out of my seat. I was holding my rosary which flew from my hand and landed on the floor. I was petrified! I looked around my home since no one was home and everything seemed normal. I was very much afraid and in horror. I called my friend Joan and she made plans for me to see Father Albert MacPherson, O.S.A., he is an Augustinian Healing Priest who travels worldwide. He has many gifts and she knew he could help me. I went to his office in Lawrence, Ma, where he is in residence. He prayed over me and doused me with Holy Water. I was told that because of the past of spending time with psychics I needed a special blessing. I was also told the devil gets very angry when you get closer to GOD and start praying a rosary a few times a day.

A week after this event my mom came to my house when I wasn't home. She picked up a religious book I had on the counter. She sat in the same chair as I did a week earlier. She was also alone and within five minutes, she felt hands wrapped around her neck. She was losing her breath and was able to drop the book and ran towards the door. She let herself out and called me as soon as she got home. She told me what had happened!

She said she felt an evil spirit was trying to strangle her. I realized at this point it was time to sell the house. I felt as if I was not wanted there and it was time to move forward. I then started blessing the house with Holy Blessed water and Holy Blessed salt as I made my way around the house. I do not know why the Lord was leading me away from the home my father had built for me. I just knew with everything breaking down around me and the evil spirit that lurked in my home it was time to move on. I did have a priest bless this home a few years ago.

UNITY FOR ALL

The Mass I had for my boss and his brother were to happen on two separate Sundays. I remember the Mass for his brother very well and thought "The Lord is speaking to me through this Homily", but I knew I could not put my stuttering on a cross because it followed me around since I was a young girl. The Homily of the day was to put all your "worries" on the "CROSS". My good friend Geri met me at Saint Williams in Tewksbury. She thought the Mass was also for me and I should pay attention to the Homily. She also told me to put this stuttering issue to sleep and read when a priest asks me too.

I have always refused and came up with the excuse of the stuttering. I didn't believe Geri and continued to do it my stubborn way. The following week was a Mass for my boss. My friend Geri met me there as well. I invited my co-workers but none of them felt they needed to be there. My boss wasn't Catholic and he did not believe in God. The Homily was done by Father John Hogan. The message of the day was Showing **"Acts of Kindness"**. It was about a boy who had a stutter and it was about a show on "Little House on the Prairie". I looked at Geri in total surprise! I believe GOD did want me there to listen to this Homily!!!

The boy was afraid to play the part because the boy had a "stutter", and Michael Landon told him to **"act it out"** and the boy decided to do it and within time his stuttering left him. I booked this Mass ninety days prior and thought this was meant for me and not for my boss.

I was meant to hear this and I had a mission to do for GOD. How selfish of me to put my own insecurity in the way of helping souls. Lord, I began to ask him for help in overcoming the biggest obstacle in my life. This story bought tears to my eyes and I thought about it for weeks. Geri was right again. I needed to change. I was holding myself back from a fear deep within my soul and when I am ready to let go then I will truly trust in GOD for everything.

UNITY FOR ALL

I was invited to Geri's house for a visit and she had beautiful religious things in her home in Wilmington, Ma. She is a devoted Catholic who loved church and Adoration and she taught me many things that would help grow in my faith. I will always be grateful for her because she had so much knowledge about our Blessed Mother. I could never learn all of it on my own. She also was very knowledgeable about the Saints.

I did not know much about the saints except for the ones who had appeared in the Eucharist. She began to tell me about Saint Therese and a Novena for the flower on the 9th day. I did not believe her or the whole novena. I said, "How can you receive the flower on the 9th day, this can not be possible". She assured me it was possible and asked me to try. She gave me a novena card and I had picked the "Yellow Rose".

I didn't think in March which was still cold and and icy it would even work. I remember praying at home and thinking this is not going to work – I will remain optimistic and just go along with Geri.

I did the novena every day and on the 9th day I called Geri before Mass and told her I did not receive the Yellow Rose. She told me the day is not over and keep praying. I went to Mass and then Adoration and I proceeded to go to my father's grave. It was a dark, cold and rainy day, also slush was still on the ground. I was praying a rosary by his grave and then telling him about the novena that I had been doing for 9 days. As I proceeded to roll up my window a wind came and I turned my head and stopped the window from going up all the way. I saw the sky open and a yellow bud landed right on my dash! I was speechless for a few seconds. I could not believe what had just happened. How can this be as there is no sun or buds on any of these trees. Where did this yellow bud come from and there were 2 to 3 buds on this green stem. I immediately called Geri and went to her house to show her. She said, I told you ! I realized at this point that GOD was showing me I can trust him as He is listening. I will never forget that day and my preference for roses will always be Yellow.

UNITY FOR ALL

It was April in 2011, and I decided it was time to put the house up for sale. It was the right decision since too much negativity was happening in the house and I believe GOD was calling me to move forward. My realtor knew I wanted to move forward and she posted the house lower since the market was depressed. We had thirteen people interested in the house within 5 hours of being online. I had to leave the house the next day and the first couple who put down a deposit came immediately. They then proceeded with an offer and we had the home inspection done.

When they had the home inspection done they found so many issues and I thought I can not possibly take down my chimney to look for more termites and changed my mind. I decided I did not want to go through all the work that was required before the real offer would follow. Several months into turning down the first offer I decided to do it again. We lost the first buyer who moved on to something else and we had other people come and look at the house, but we did not have any interest as we did the first time. I decided to put Saint Joseph in the ground. I buried him upside down in the front walkway and purposely put a seventy pound angel of concrete over him. I was certain he would stay there and if I needed to find him all I had to do was move the concrete angel and dig about 5" below.

Time was passing and people were coming, but every comment was the house needed too much work. We then reduced the house back to the original price and still had heard the comments. I remember telling my friend Joan about putting Saint Joseph in the ground, and she told me to take him out and to pray to Lady Fatima. She said you need to put two flower pots on the front steps and pray to Lady Fatima. I didn't understand why and thought I had better do what she tells me. I proceeded to moving the cherub concrete statue off of Saint Joseph and I dug down 5 inches. I kept digging. I dug and looked and dug all around this cherub. I could not find Saint Joseph. I even called my friend Roseann to help me. We could not find him.

UNITY FOR ALL

I looked at the ground near where I had him and there were no signs that he had been dug up. I thought about it and knew I had put him there and some how he was gone. I then put back the dirt and the statue was back in it's place. I went to a wedding and asked if I could take home the two flower pots and had permission. I put them on the front steps.

I then prayed to Mary and said, "Dear Mary, if my house should sell within thirty days, I will personally go to Fatima and thank you". Keep in mind I had never left the country before this. I did not even own a passport.

My son was leaving to go to Florida with his girlfriend and her family for two weeks. During that time we had a buyer who wanted to look at the house. I had a feeling deep down it would sell when my son was away.

The buyer was very interested in this house. They had done an immediate house inspection. The offer came back and I was moving forward. This was happening so fast, and this time I knew it was going to work. I also realized I had to go to Portugal as promised. I knew I would take Roseann which will make it a very good trip. I offered her the trip and money if she helped me move all these things from my home. I had many obstacles blocking this move and it was not as easy as I hoped it would be. The town needed clearance on the property and the documents were lost. My father had passed away in 1997, and the engineer who worked on our land also passed away. We were supposed to close on 9/1/2011, and as it turned out we closed on 9/9/2011. What happened was one long stressful episode after another and I knew I had to move forward and be faced with every obstacle that was put in front of me.

Then they said my tennis court was not completely on my property. It was on the Lowell line and had to be dug up. I had to hire a land surveyor and I did not have the money upfront. The land surveyor said I could pay him after the house closed. As it turned out the tennis court was on the line. I had to go before the planning board to get the paperwork that was stalling this move from happening. I also had to move heavy poles out of my backyard and off of my property. I had my son's friends use a dolly which I had and move each one from the back of the shed to the front of the driveway.

It was no easy task and each one weighed anywhere from 75 pounds to 325 pounds. When they were done with the last one the dolly wheels broke and became flat. They left them in a pile at the bottom of my driveway. I looked at Roseann and wondered how I was going to get them into my van at that time. She looked at me and said we have to hire a professional to move them.

I then realized all I had to do was pray to the Holy Spirit for strength. I looked at Roseann and told her I was going to pray to the Holy Spirit for strength. She said there was no way we could both move them. If my sons friends needed a dolly to move them and now we do not have a dolly, what can we do? I just knew in my soul we could do it with the Lord's help. I walked over to one of them and blessed myself and recited, "Father", "Son", and "Holy Spirit". I had strength and picked up the first pole which was not heavy and carried it to my van and put it in the back. Roseann was speechless as she watched me do this one after another. I told her the Lord had given me the strength to do it. She was shocked. I asked her to move one and she could not move it one inch off the ground. I then proceeded one after another and we took them to a big trash bin and I had the strength at this site to get them out of my van and stand them up straight at this trash bin. We did this about three times and the last trip I knew would be the hardest. I had one pole left and it was the biggest out of the eight. It must have weighed 320 pounds. I was to lift and drag it to the back of my van. I knew picking it up would require two of us. I blessed myself and prayed and asked Roseann to stand behind me and pick up the pole on the count of three. She looked at me like I was crazy and I told her to trust in GOD. He was going to do all the work.

On the count of three she picked up her end and said it weighed less than five pounds and it went into my van very easily. As we stood there in disbelief I knew GOD was working with us to get everything out. He even gave me the strength to pull it out of my van myself and stand it upright at the bin. I remember we worked one time all night long I was never tired. I knew I had to clean out sixteen rooms in order to meet the closing date. If we were not giving items away we were packing them up for storage. I had to get two large storages to hold the items I was keeping and everything else was donated. I remember looking back at all of this and realizing the LORD was with me 100 Percent in that move. I was moving out all night and heading to work the next day and then coming home to pack again.

I could not afford to pay the gas bill and we were taking freezing showers. I prayed to GOD and an apartment became available in Tyngsboro, Ma. I took it for my son and he went there while I continued to move items from the house and get it ready for closing day.

I do not know how all of this was done but, it happened. I never had a yard sale we donated everything and I kept only our heirlooms which were the most important of everything. My son kept his music and clothing and I kept clothes and heirlooms. I also kept my mom's paintings and jewelry. Everything else was to give away and I felt very happy in doing it this way. I had a friend from high school come over several days before my closing. He took the basketball hoop and other things. My friend was telling him that I could never find Saint Joseph and he asked her if you could not find Saint Joseph, then who is that standing up next to the statue! She immediately asked me and I went to see and it was Saint Joseph. He reappeared. I picked him up and put him in a box for my storage in Tyngsboro.

There he was and I have no idea how long he was there. When I looked for him months prior he was not there and he reappeared two days before the house was closing!

UNITY FOR ALL

I remember waking up the next morning and going to work after being up all night getting the house ready for the closing. My van was full of items which needed to get to storage and my closing was in the afternoon. I picked up my friend Roseann and we went to meet the lawyers. I met the buyers and they assured me they loved the house. We signed papers in the afternoon and I was free of the burdens of the house and on to a new chapter in my life. I never had any regrets and never looked back. I believe that house was a dark period in my life and I needed to move forward and accomplish more for GOD.

I was now living in an apartment about 810 square feet. I never lived in an apartment in my life. This was certainly a change for me and my son, Andrew. We had to do our laundry downstairs and I enjoyed this very much.

I had lots of money in the bank since I did not have a mortgage on the house. I still kept my mini van which was slowly letting go. The transmission was stuck and I was told it would let go at any moment. I felt I should keep it until it does let go and look for a house in my spare time. I did look at some houses but nothing really interested me. The woman who lived across the hall from me was selling all of her possessions. She had some type of rare cancer. She said she had some rare disease and the chemo did not work.

The fellow upstairs was Christian and he asked me to pray for him. The woman across the hall had a very dark apartment and all her blinds were closed during the day. She had skulls everywhere and was selling a lot of things. I remember walking in and hugging her and blessing her with Saint Raphael Holy Blessed oil. She was completely white and thin and told me she was preparing her funeral. I prayed for her every day and also in Adoration. I lived there for a year and she never passed away.

A few months passed and my friend Roseann reminded me it was time we went to Portugal. I told her I felt afraid of this flight as I never left the country.

She told me I had made a promise to Mary. She was right. We needed to go and so I had my passport done and booked our flights. We were leaving on the 9th of November, 2011 and coming back on the 15th . We had no idea where we were going and what to even see accept Lady Fatima. I said we will let the Holy Spirit guide us and trust He will lead.

The flight was very smooth and peaceful. I have flown with Roseann in the past and all my flights with her were always at peace. We landed in Saint Miguel Island and then soon after to Lisbon, Portugal. We rented a car and drove to Fatima, Portugal. We had no idea what to expect since it was our first time in this country and my first time in another country. I booked our room at the Domis Pacis hotel which was across the street from the Basilica.

The first day we attended Mass, then we went to the Adoration Chapel. I remember praying to Jesus and saw a boy staring at me in the Eucharist from 25 to 30 feet from the altar. I asked Jesus if he could show Roseann what he was showing me.

I am always telling Roseann what Jesus shows me and I thought what a blessing for her to see what I see. She then proceeded to tell me she saw something in the Eucharist. She started staring as I have done so many times and admitted to seeing a boy's face. I told her I saw the exact same thing! I was so thankful Jesus gave her the gift to see too. We also found out the next day while praying in the garden the Angel of Peace was the same boy's face we both saw in the Eucharist. That was a confirmation for me to know he was with us on this Journey. We woke up the next day and went to breakfast.

The day was 11-11-11, (November 11, 2011). I remember sitting with Roseann in the dining room of the Domis Pacis hotel. There were three people who we met and started talking to us. They thought I was part of the Blue Army. I never even heard of the Blue Army International until meeting them. We met Veronica from Fuji Island, and the President of the Blue Army International from Puerto Rico and another Ambassador from

UNITY FOR ALL

England. They asked me if I wanted to join and I told them I was there for Jesus and I did a novena and because my house sold I came to thank Lady Fatima. They were fascinated by my love for Jesus and my devotion to Adoration. They insisted I meet Nuno who runs the Blue Army and his office is around the other side of the building. I said I would love to, but not that day. I would meet him another day. They arranged it and I stayed and spoke with Veronica. She told me she was an ambassador for the Blue Army and does talks at several countries. She also told me she stuttered quite bad and got over it when she started doing her presentations. She was a mom of five children and this was her mission in life. She told me I must not be afraid to speak and to put my stuttering behind me as a cross.

She also said she had no money and would love to buy a Statue for an African church because they did not have one. I told her I can give her some money and take her to the store to buy the statue. She was also afraid of rain and it started to rain out. She was petrified of rain and had anxiety over it. She took my hand as it started to rain and we walked out to the shrine to pray. I noticed she had on a watch named "Rocky" and I had a big black lab named "Rocky". She gave me the watch since I gave her $125.00. We then went to the store and that was where she bought a 3' statue for the church in Africa. She left the next day and that was when I received the call to meet with Nuno on the 14th. I walked to his office with Roseann and we stayed for about two hours. I told him my love for Jesus and all that had happened to me. I even asked him if he knew what 0512 meant? He said all he could think of is **"a thousand people flock to Fatima"** on May 12th, to prepare for May 13th. It was a beautiful day and he gave me some books and I bought some video's and some jewelry. I was so happy to have met him as well as Anna. At that time Anna told me her grandmother was alive when the sun came down in Fatima in 1917. I remember Nuno asking me if I were interested in the Blue Army and I told him I stuttered and I could never do public speaking.

UNITY FOR ALL

I tried to adopt the puppy we saw every night at the Basilica, but the town said it would take six months to get him out of quarantine. Roseann and I were feeding this puppy we saw nightly at the shrine the whole time we were there. He kept reappearing and sitting by the beautiful Lady Fatima each night. I took pictures of him and asked others who went shortly after us if they had seen him and no one ever saw this dog again. If I ever get the chance to go back I would like to rescue one of the dogs which run stray there. They are all beautiful and I was told they come from the farmers nearby.

Chapter Three

It was now 2012, and I began spending lots of time in Adoration on the weekends. The heat from just sitting in front of the Blessed Sacrament was so very beautiful. My body was at complete peace and I had no worries at all. I was told by many I had a glow and my life began to be consumed by Adoration. I was now also working full time and was on fire with prayer life and consumed by meeting people at Adoration on the weekends. It seemed my life was different in so many ways. I looked at life different and I wanted to be with Jesus every chance I had. I felt this bond in my soul that was trusting and loving and not like anything I had ever felt in my life. Imagine having happy thoughts 24 hours a day and feeling so much in love with GOD you want to explode just at the mention of his name. I kept thinking, I wish I could spend all my time in a church and be with Jesus all the time. I understood fully that being in work meant just passing time and being with Jesus in Adoration was where I wanted to be all the time. A real purpose of life. As I began to look at people I realized that some souls had no idea what was going on in the spiritual world. They live in the world and are of the world. I did not want to be part of the world. I wanted to be with Him in Adoration which is where I felt amazing.

I started praying more consistently for souls who are lost in this world and for conversions. I felt if I could help others come to love Jesus the way He had changed me, maybe they too, will find everlasting love.

Several months went by and now we are in May 2012. It was May 12, 2012, and I was going to look at a house with Jody Germano my Realtor, and my mother. My mother's name is Pauline. She had been living in a townhouse in Tewksbury, and was not very happy. I was living in an apartment and wanted to come closer to home. We decided to look at this enormous home in Tewksbury, as it turned out my uncle built the house originally in the 70's, and lived next door until the 90's when he bought a townhouse near the airport in Tewksbury.

When we got to the house I was speaking to the home owner. I knew her from the past. My son took Origami from her husband at the Tewksbury Public Library. My realtor went upstairs and said, "Suzanne wait till you come up here". I decided to see what she wanted me to see. As I walked up the stairs I saw her – Lady Fatima statue all wood and she stood about 38" high. The date was **0512**. I thought how can this be, was God preparing me to see her on **May 12th 2012?** I was in shock and I immediately went down stairs and asked the homeowner about the statue. She told me her aunt had a late calling in life and went to Fatima and had her made. She said if I buy the house I can have her. I bought a townhouse instead and called her up and she said she would sell her to me. I gave her a check of $300.00, US currency dollars and she was mine. I promised her I would take good care of her and that I had a ministry. I also said everyone will know how I came to her and that she was special to me. I believe GOD wanted me to have her. She cried while I said these things to her and I gave her a big hug. As I left her I felt sad for her having to move and I knew she wanted to stay in her home. I was thankful GOD made the connection and I prayed for her every day after for a long time. Jesus had shown me another miracle and my faith and love for him was growing daily. Thank you Jesus!!!

I bought a townhouse and passed papers on July 26th, 2012. I was happy to be settled and in a new place. It felt peaceful to be there and I immediately loved the patio which was all fenced in. I put in seventy or so yellow bulbs in memory of Saint Therese on the back patio. I knew I would do this immediately and it would give me something to look forward to each spring. I never thought I would even be in a townhouse but, this townhouse I felt drawn to and I kept going back over and over again prior to the purchase. We are close to the highway, but there is a great sense of peace here. I love all my neighbors very much and my son and I have grown to love the community here. It is the half-way point to two churches which I belong to and all my friends live around me. They have no rules here and allowed me to put up a brick wall out front as well as put any religious things I wanted out front and out back. I realized I was in a good place and one where I can be free to do what I want without being judged.

UNITY FOR ALL

<u>Chapter Four</u>

One evening while praying in my room I heard, "**I am with you always**". This came in a whisper as I lay there ready to recite my rosary. I realized as loud as the noise from the highway is in my bedroom Jesus is still whispering to me and I can hear him no matter what. I longed to hear his voice in my home. I thought each time it will be more beautiful than the previous. He said in another voice, "**You must do "God's" work and blessings will come upon you and your family forever**". I kept telling him I can't follow him because I have a job and I must continue to pay for my son's education so he can have a good start in life. I thought I had been doing his work by meeting people at Adoration on the weekends. As I said it was a full time job and I was travelling between many different Chapels. I found myself being in outside sales, talking about Adoration to customers. I felt the Holy Spirit come upon me many times and I was not speaking, he was speaking through me. I also had some Ministry Cards made and started passing them out weekly and dropping them off at Chapels. I wanted others to read my story and direct them to other Chapels.

I am sitting in Adoration and I hear the word, "MOSES", over and over again. I again had to ask what that meant. I continued to see people in the Eucharist and at work one of the people I saw in the Eucharist we hired, who ended up coming to Adoration with me. It appeared Jesus was showing me souls and either I would meet them or they would meet me and hear about Adoration. I was also told to give GOD all the glory and never stop thanking him for these gifts.

One of my friends, Mike Spinelli, also has a ministry and Evangelizes on Saint Margaret Mary. Mike does Enthronements of the Sacred Heart in homes of the faithful.

Mike had just completed the novena for the Sacred Heart of Jesus and was now ready to have Jesus Christ Enthroned in his own home. He invited me to this event and I decided to bring my friend Joan with me.

Mike asked me to be present since I spend a lot of time in Adoration and I would like to see how this process was done. I agreed and noticed that Mike had to do a lot of talking before he hung the picture on the wall. He had a hard time in doing this and broke down in tears in front of his family.

I felt so bad for him and I remember saying, I hope he doesn't ask me to do this I don't want to have to give a speech like this. As I watched him do this speech it took him at least five minutes to gather himself together before he could finish.

When it was done he looked at me and I said, "There is no way I could do that. It would be too much talking".

He assured me it's a beautiful way to Introduce Jesus to your home and the graces are just amazing . Mike has been a devoted Catholic his entire life and knows the bible quite well. He is also most eager to help anyone with any questions about Jesus or any saint. Mike is a good soul and always willing to help me.

If I recall back in 2010, it was my devotion to Adoration that got Mike to do Adoration. He had a calling for the rosary and this is how the two of us got together. Mike had been a good friend to my parents for over fifty years.

Mike had a travel agency which he sold to Vacation.com. He was now retired and living in New Hampshire. He had traveled much of his entire life and knew all religions quite well. The Bible he also knew very well and taught classes on it at his church in Hampton, NH.

One could certainly learn a lot from Mike. I have gone with him to Adoration a few times on Wednesday evening at 9:00 PM.

Mike could never understand how I could sit on the hard pew for hours, and never complain. I admired Mike's involvement with GOD, and the saints, especially Saint Padre Pio.

Mike asked me several months later to have the Sacred Heart Enthroned in my home. He suggested to me that I find the DVD and watch it. I agreed I would do it after I watched the DVD, but I had to find the DVD first. Mike thought that EWTN had it but when I went online it was sold out. I went to Amazon and it too was sold out. I did an extensive search and none were available.

I then prayed to the Holy Spirit and on the 2nd day one became available at Amazon and from a Church in New Jersey. I ordered it and waited for it to come in. I remember watching the DVD and within thirty minutes I knew I must have this done in my home. I immediately contacted Mike Spinelli and told him I would do it. I also chose the nine day novena and not the three day novena. He told me everyone does the three day, and I insisted on the nine day. He emailed me the prayers and I was excited about having it done. I remember the first night was easy as it was a Saturday night. The next night I remembered there was a lot more praying and I had better go upstairs earlier.

I was very tired too and thinking I might fall asleep I asked GOD to help me. I remember walking upstairs. It was quite late and I had been out all day and was very tired. I thought, "How can I pray tonight I am so tired". The minute I crossed into my bedroom I was wide awake. It's as if I just woke up and had slept for ten hours".

I was also very happy and joyful while reciting these prayers. I did all the praying and went to bed. The next day I awoke and felt at peace and lots of Love was surrounding me. I went to work and came home late again. My experiences from the previous night was repeated and continued for the rest of the week.

UNITY FOR ALL

Each night I found myself heading upstairs at about 11:15 PM, feeling very tired but when I made the cross between the hall to my bedroom this burst of energy took over and I was filled with the Holy Spirit and so happy and joyful.

The day prior to the event I went out with my friend and told her all about my renewed energy at night while praying the novena. She thought that alone was some sort of a miracle in itself. That day we also saw three animals all in white. We went to a pet store in NH and they had a white quaker parrot. They told me how rare they are and they never had one in before. Then we went to a farm and saw pure white turkeys, and later to a fair where one of the people brought a pure white dog. I saw 3 white animals all in one day this was very strange.

The next day the Sacred Heart was Enthroned in my home and everyone came including my mom.

I read the Enthronement and never stuttered once and had a peaceful loving day. I never felt so good and loved and was happy to have experienced such a beautiful feeling. My Sacred Heart of Jesus is proudly hung in my hallway heading up the staircase and Mike Spinelli bought the picture for me and had it framed.

<u>Chapter Five</u>

It was Lent again and March of 2014, I felt a great peace come upon me at work. It's as if the Holy Spirit is not only with me but in me. I could not understand though why he was coming to my office. I felt him many times at my home but never at the office. I remember being at my desk and this feeling of a great peace came upon me. I thought why isn't my boss in here and tell me he can't hear me on the phone. He was sitting in the next office and here I am in a great peace as if I walked twenty miles and time was standing still. This day especially I felt the presence for four hours. I was in love with Love in my office. I was in a rested place with an ultimate peace at the office. Thank you GOD! I love having you here with me. I knew I had to make phone calls and forced myself to do it all the while feeling His presence was the ultimate feeling in the world. I watched my boss who was occupied on his computer during the four hour presence in my office. It's as if the two of us were under the direction of the Lord to be at peace and enjoy the moment. This was a miracle that he did not come in my office because we worked together every day and this was one day the two of us were occupied completely and neither one bothered the other.

A few days later my boss came in my office and was talking about furniture sales. He said if I had furniture sales my margins would double and he wanted to teach me how to sell furniture. I agreed. The basic training lasted twenty minutes or so and I went back to my office. As I sat there I called upon the Holy Spirit to help me. I then proceeded to open the phone book and I never took leads from the phone book. My leads came from business to business on foot.

I was not afraid to do cold calling door to door. In fact, I loved it and it helped me so much to build my confidence.

There I was in the phone book and my inner thoughts were to call an HVAC Company. I didn't know why but, I did. I picked one out and spoke with the CEO of the company.

He told me he just built out a new space in his office and is in need of furniture. He even spoke with a company in Waltham who was coming out to measure in a few weeks. I asked for the appointment as well and got in a week earlier.

I told my boss I just landed an appointment with an HVAC Company for furniture and it was the work of the Holy Spirit. My boss looked at me like I was crazy and I was telling him the truth. I may have made that appointment, but the choice to call came from the Holy Spirit. Besides, we just spoke of him asking me to sell furniture to boost up my sales. We went on the appointment a week later and the customer booked $6,000, US, plus worth of desks and other pieces. He was right it was a great way to boost up my sales and I thanked the Holy Spirit for helping me. This company turned out to be one of our newest customers for all of furniture and supplies. I gave all the glory to GOD and did not realize what was about to happen in the months to come. My boss trusted me to go out and promote furniture to anyone who wanted it and realized I caught on so quick all of them would be easy sales from this day forward.

I started praying to the Holy Spirit to help me in all work related duties. All my appointments were easy once I could get the soul on the phone. I knew while on the phone that I would get the appointment before it was even booked. I trusted everything to GOD.

The feeling of peace came upon me prior to the call and during the call. Many of the customers said they never let anyone in the door but felt while speaking with me over the phone something told them to let me come. I did not realize that GOD was working me while on the road too.

I called on an environmental company in Woburn, Mass. I spoke with Steve Fleming, the President and CEO. He took the appointment over the phone. He then called a few days later and had to re-schedule. A coworker of his asked him why he had me coming since he already had a vendor he liked. Steve told his employee that something inside of him told him to let me come in. He himself did not know what to think of it and trusted his conscience. I arrived in the afternoon of a Friday. These meetings usually go for fifteen to thirty minutes depending on how much a customer is willing to share of their current purchase.

I walked in the door and he took me back to his office. His building was on the 4th floor and his office looked over the whole parking lot. We started talking about office supplies and within fifteen minutes of the meeting I felt the presence of the Holy Spirit. This was the first time this has ever happened to me while with a client. I did not know what to do and just felt this great peace come upon me right in our meeting. I proceeded to ask him if he was Catholic. I don't know why I even asked that, but it did come out. He told me he was Catholic and had not been to Adoration in twenty years. He then told me he went to Catholic High School, Catholic College and met his wife at college who was also Catholic. He thought Adoration was only during Easter.

I told him I was there to sell him office supplies, but he wanted to know more about Adoration. Again, I felt this was unprofessional of me. He insisted I go on.

I started to tell him about my conversion and how Adoration is a big part of my life and many healings come from trusting GOD. He told me about his wife's friend who has a brain tumor and had just six months left to live. I invited her to Adoration and to also come to a healing service in Reading, Mass. He and I sat there and talked and talked and talked. He asked me why I did not do public talks and I told him I am very fearful of public speaking, and my love for GOD is simply amazing and I was in love with him very much.

UNITY FOR ALL

He assured me my talking to him was a message he needed to hear as he was thinking of GOD, but did not go to church for a while.

He bought a chair from me because he felt I gave him three hours of my time in talks of God's love for him. I left there feeling as if this appointment was all for GOD. I was so excited walking out to my car and hoped I made a difference in his life.

> **Peter 1.8 You have not seen him, yet you love him, and still without seeing him you believe in him and so are already filled with a joy so glorious that it cannot be described. (catholic online-catholic.org)**

Steve wrote to me a few hours later and told me when he got in his car and drove home he pulled over off the highway and realized GOD sent me to him. He prayed a rosary in his car on the side of the road and went back to church.

He realized I had a big call in evangelzing Adoration and this message needed to get out to the world. We continued to talk about GOD every time we were on the phone and I did meet Jen shortly afterwards. Her story is another miracle as well which I will talk about later.

During the next week more GOD coincidences started to happen. At each and every visit I felt the presence of the Holy Spirit. I had no control over what was happening to me and all I could do was pray for the souls around me and hope GOD touched them in some way possible. I knew he was using me for a mission and if this was what he wanted me to do he would come upon me and have control over the time he needed.

I was sent out to meet a company in Cambridge, Mass in the afternoon. This was unusual for me since I did most of my meetings in Cambridge in the morning, but this appointment was at 3:00 P.M. I figured if I stay for an hour and then went home by back roads I would not hit much traffic. When I arrived at this appointment which was in Cambridge, I met with the buyer. She was a petite woman and she worked with a company in Engineering for a long time. She sat behind the desk and when I walked in I was in front of a window peeking in and she forgot all about our appointment and said she would speak with me anyway. I told her I would be brief and wanted to drop off our catalogs and give her some samples.

As we were talking she decided to come around to the front of where I was sitting and show me the copy paper which she had been buying from another supplier. When she came out I sensed the feeling of her soul. It was as if I was in her body and she had a very sad look upon her face.

Within a split second of her sitting down in front of me I felt the presence of the Holy Spirit on my right.

I knew He was sitting right next to me and He came with such peace. I started to ask her what denomination she was and she said Catholic.

She also broke down and started crying right in front of me. I told her not to worry as God was with us. She told me she was very upset with God. I began to listen to her speak. She had not been to church in a very long time and I asked her if she ever went to Adoration. She told me she never heard about Adoration in her life. I told her how Adoration had helped me and where I was in my faith and about my conversion. She told me she did not have her car and she let her brother-in-law take it to bring his wife to work and him to his job as well. She had been walking to work every day. She had no way of getting to church or to a chapel. I realized we had been talking for a few hours since I arrived at 3:00 PM, and was off at 4:00 PM, but now it was 6:00

PM. She bought some supplies from me since we spent more than two hours talking about God.

She told me she would love to go to Adoration and I offered to bring her some Saturday that I was free and I invited her to a future healing Mass with Father Albert MacPherson, and she said her brother-in-law would benefit since he had severe backaches. I did pick her up a few weeks after we met and we did go to Adoration together. I took her to Saint Williams in Tewksbury. We went to the chapel and I immediately let Jesus know as soon as we arrived that she was here to see you and she had confession for you. She only stayed a few minutes before running out and I went out to find her. I found her under a bush in deep sorrow. I never experienced anything like this before.

She told me it was so painful to sit in His presence and I suggested she speak to Father Andrew, my Pastor. She did not feel comfortable and asked if I would mind taking her to a coffee shop. I told her absolutely and we proceeded. As I arrived again I mentioned she would feel so much better if she would speak with a priest. She was not ready. We sat down and talked for many many hours. I felt helpless and listened. I kept praying to the Holy Spirit to help me.

What words could I offer that would give her peace and healing. She had been hanging on to so much from her past and all she had to do was confess. I knew if she saw a priest she would feel so much better.

I realized God was using me to bring her and others like her back to him. If it meant I was to listen and console each time I would for my love for Him. I also had a real sense on what a priest does and appreciated his role more and more as a parishioner. In time, she did go to Confession and she was seeking Adoration in her town of Belmont, Mass. She found out they had it one hour a week. I pray one day the Pastor opens more hours for his parishioners and maybe she will volunteer an hour a week and more souls will join her and also take an hour. If one soul benefits imagine how many more souls would also enjoy His presence, I thought!

UNITY FOR ALL

One day while at work my boss wanted me to visit an account that was past due. I never did this before and was apprehensive. He assured me since it was my account and he did not have the relationship so therefore he wanted me to go. Our accounts payable department had exhausted all methods of getting them to call us back and since it was my account I was told I had to collect the debt. I was to show up and ask for the check. I did just that.

When I arrived I asked to speak with the VP of Finance. They had me sit in a conference room for more than thirty minutes and wait. As I sat and waited and waited he finally came down stairs. I introduced myself to him and he sat down. I felt the presence at this time which was very strong. I knew the Holy Spirit was with me and I did not second guess anything. I felt this deep deep peace as I was speaking to him. I began to ask him about the check which his company owes us and the four months backlog on receiving funds. He assured me his company has some cash issues and we are on a list of vendors to pay. I also told him not to worry since we never charge late fees or interest to our vendors. As we talked back and forth I began to talk about Easter and then Adoration. He looked right at me and said, "God sent you here"! I then said, "My boss sent me here". He told me his mother is very sick with cancer. I told him not to worry, and that there was a healing Mass with Father Albert. I also suggested he attend an hour with his mother in Adoration and give this cancer to Jesus. We talked of Adoration and GOD for the following hour. He then promised me he would make sure the next check they received he would cut us a check of what he owed in full. He apologized for not paying us sooner. I asked him if he wanted to receive my ministry card so he can follow my schedule of where I was and where to find me. He said, "Isn't this what the Apostles did with Jesus?" I will follow you! We went outside to my van and I gave him a ministry card. He gave me a big hug in the parking lot and told me he was going to church to thank God for my visit. He did send our company a check in full within two weeks. Praise GOD! My boss was in shock we were paid so fast and I never told him what happened. I just assured him in God's time we would be paid.

UNITY FOR ALL

I was then invited by Father Albert to attend a special Mass at his church and the Bishop, "Sean O'Malley" would be present.

I invited my friend Denise to join me. Father Albert resides at Saint Mary of the Assumption, in Lawrence, Mass. He travels a lot and most of the year conducting healing Masses, parish missions, and pilgrimages. This church is magnificent. I visited once prior in 2011, when I needed a special blessing, but at that time the church was under construction and I did not see it.

When we arrived and opened the door we felt the love which was very strong. It was something I have not felt in any other church in my life. The people welcomed us immediately. We loved the altar and the huge ceilings. I thought this Church is so beautiful and it is close to my home I can come more often. I also loved the Adoration Chapel which is street level. The people here are so loving and welcoming. I felt like I was part of their life immediately, yet I did not know anyone. The ceremony began and the music was so beautiful as was the service. I felt as if these people were my family as well. I especially liked the part when we said the Lord's prayer and afterwards the family left the pews and went from pew to pew hugging each other. It was something and the priest comes off of the Pulpit and into the isle to praise and worship God. No script in their hands they just spoke freely!

We were invited by Father Albert for tea, crackers and cheese in the dining room. We followed him downstairs to the rectory. The kitchen was beautiful and the dining room was very big. As we sat and ate my ceasar salad which I made that morning, we also had tea and cheese with crackers. It was simple yet elegant.

I spoke to other parishioners as well about my love of Adoration and we shared our stories for the next few hours or so. Father then asked me about landscaping and how he had planted so much on the property. I mentioned to him that my father was a builder and I had done some work at my previous home and my love for the hobby as well. He had a lot of work to do at this parish but funds were always an issue. He also needed help with the grounds and I offered to help him. He asked me to come back the following week and I told him I would help him anyway I could. Little did I know this offering would be a big project in the future. I knew in my heart that God was calling me to Saint Mary's in Lawrence, Mass. The following week I met Father Albert at Saint Mary's. He cooked me scrambled eggs for breakfast. I will admit they were very good as was his tea. He proceeded to tell me where we are going to plant two bushes in the back of the church. We went out there and he showed me all the rose bushes which he planted in the last ten years. He also showed me the grounds. We planted two bushes out back which he had bought for the church.

We then went to Mass that evening as well. I felt drawn to go back and help again. He took me out front and showed me the weeding he had to do when he came back from his summer vacation. Father Albert spent years pulling weeds, removing old trees, pruning others and planted forty trees, as well as many rose bushes. I knew in my heart I could help him and offered to buy the materials if he could help me do all the landscaping. He agreed. We made plans to borrow the church pickup truck for the following week.

We went to the landscaping store in Plaistow, NH and got the stones and Father Albert would get the ground ready while I was at work and at night I would work at Saint Mary's until midnight until our projects were all done. I invited my good friend Mike Spinelli to come see this church and what I was about to do. I asked him if he would help me with splitting the bill of materials and he agreed. I was to do all the laboring as well with Father Albert and Mike and I would split the cost of the materials. Mike also fell in love with the church and I introduced him to Father Carlos. Mike wanted to do more for the church and offered to buy the rosary beads and give them to Father Carlos to pass out to the parishioners. Mike had a ministry as well and he loved the Blessed Virgin Mary deeply.

The work lasted about 3 months. I worked after work and sometimes all day Saturday. I remember going to work all day in my day job and coming home and changing and heading to Saint Mary's to work till midnight. The Lord gave me the strength. I invited Roseann to help me one day and she climbed into the pickup truck and shoveled over 100 times into the wheelbarrow where Father Albert dumped it into an area where I spread the rocks by hand.

Each truck load weighed about 1,000 pounds of rocks which were small but heavy. We did a total of 14 trips to the landscaping store in Plaistow, NH. What surprised me was I had so much energy at night I was never tired even after working ten hour days. I contributed this to spending time in Adoration before I started helping Father Albert. I had no pain and no tired feelings. I felt energized and at peace. The grounds were coming together and everything looked so beautiful.

We planted more rose bushes and black eyed susies out front, first we put down red stones and in front of the church we put down white stones. Father Albert removed the top soil and we found new places to put everything. He taught me "Waste Not Want Not". I recited this over and over as we worked. Many times working in silence I said a rosary as I went on with my work. I was very content there and knew I wanted to be there.

Philippians 4:13 – I have strength for everything through him who empowers me.(usccb.org)

I felt drawn to Saint Mary's and the more I did the more I wish I had lived there. I wish it was my home and I wanted to make her pretty. The parishioners saw me working there night after night and began thanking me. Whatever was asked of me to do I went along with it and did it. I knew I was doing God's work and no matter what this made my soul feel loved. Father Albert told me he was going on summer vacation and asked me if I would water all the flowers and I told him I would. I didn't realize at the time the big undertaking it would be, but I agreed. I drove to the church three times a week after work, dinner or another prayer service and watered for an hour or more each time.

UNITY FOR ALL

Sometimes I was there till 10:00 and 11:00 PM. I wanted to be sure everything was watered well and we had a very hot summer.

When Father Albert came back he noticed everything was in full bloom and there were no weeds he had to pull. Everything was just as pretty or prettier before he left. I had a marvelous summer praying in front of the church and behind the church. When he came back we both thought of a bench out front. I started to price out benches in a trek material. I had to pay for this on my own.

I looked and found one which was expensive. I did not want to take the money out of my bank account so I prayed about it. I trusted God would help me and the bench did arrive. Father Albert made a place for it in front of the church and he paid for the mortar and the marble piece which was to go in front of this beautiful bench which I had bought for the church. He also put the six foot bench together with a few other parishioners, and Father Albert and I mixed the top cement and put the bench in the ground. We then went to the patio store and bought several bags of small white marble chips and laid them down as well. It was done. Our project was almost complete. We laid the marble piece into the ground as well. The very next day I went to work and a woman called in from a referral. She asked for me. She told me she was referred to me and needed office furniture for a new office. I went to her office and she bought enough to cover the bench which I just paid for myself. I knew God heard my prayers. The bench was now all paid for in full. We sat on the bench and talked about all the work we had done over the course of six months. As I began to go to the church I admired the labor and the team effort in making such a holy place beautiful. I realized I was called there to help them. I still see many other projects I would like to do and time and money are the biggest issues.

My love for this church will always be the same. The Pastor plays a big part in this church and his people. Father Carlos Urbina is an awesome priest and if you are blessed enough to attend a Mass he is celebrating and hear his Homily you would enjoy it. I have invited many souls and each one have said,

UNITY FOR ALL

"wow – such a powerful message". I realized this was the beginning of my projects there and I was going to attend this Chapel as often as I could too.

Several months later the priests all came together and wanted to cook me a meal for all the hard work and for my birthday. Father Joe Murray, who at the time was a brother, now a priest, did the cooking. He made me calmari in a spaghetti sauce with a delicious salad and strawberry shortcake. I felt so loved and appreciated. I invited Mike Spinelli and Father Carlos read us scripture all evening. It was such a beautiful evening and one I will treasure for a lifetime.

I went to visit the DeColores book store in Salem, NH. I enjoy this store very much and bought my first bible here in 2009. The owner Adele and her employees arc so helpful and Holy people. They sell lots of Christian items in this store and everyone that I have met there have found something for most Christians.

It was getting late and they were closing the store and I nccded to buy my items and go home. I remember talking with the gal at the register when this woman walked in the store. They asked her if they can help her with anything. She mentioned she was looking for angels. She was actually on her way to see a psychic and told this to us! I told her that this is the last place she should be going and not to go see the psychic. I proceeded to tell her about Adoration. She never heard of Adoration. I knew time was an issue and gave her my ministry card and asked her to reach out to me via Facebook after she read my story on www.letthelightinme.com. We departed and when I got home she emailed me.

She read my story and I invited her to Saint Mary's in Lawrence. She agreed to come. We sat and prayed in Adoration for an hour. Then we went to Mass. Keep in mind I never met Ann Marie prior to the Christian Store. We were total strangers, and now friends. Ann Marie told me she felt a wonderful peace at Adoration and she loved it. I mentioned that her church had Adoration too, it was on Mondays and she could go and she

UNITY FOR ALL

ended up taking the hour 1-2:00 PM every Monday. This went on for three years till she decided to pop in when she could since she had other obligations on Mondays at that time. She felt Adoration was really helping her and she encouraged me to speak about it to a wider audience. I told her I had a fear of public speaking and I had a stutter which would come out from that fear. She kept telling me if I could do it the Lord would reach more people. She said Adoration has helped her with so much and I realized God was continuing to use me to help other souls.

I was attending a healing Mass in Reading which Father Albert asked me to come. I invited all the new souls which had been in contact with me the last few months. Everyone wanted to go and those people need healings.

We all are in a broken world and it's important to acknowledge that there is help out there. If you are open to receive a gift all you have to do is come and open your heart and receive. My boss was even coming with his girlfriend and he wasn't even Catholic.

I remember in the parking lot a woman came up to me, her name was Jen. She was the girl Steve Fleming mentioned to me that had a brain tumor and had just six months to live. She began to tear a little telling me about her cancer and she was on chemo at the time. I felt so sad for her and knew she was sent to me to pray with her and for her. Her mom came also and Jen was seeking a miracle.

We walked in the church and I invited her to meet Father Albert. I told her when you go up to the altar to receive God's blessings always open up your palms and keep your arms out front to receive. I also told her some of us will fall back and that is the Holy Spirit working within. I told her for years I fought that feeling of wanting to fall back and one day when I was up at the altar and the Eucharist was on the altar in the monstrance I fell back and was slain in the spirit for at least twenty minutes. It was very beautiful experience, but never as deep as when I meditate in Adoration. However, each time it is a very peaceful and joyous experience. Many of my friends attend these healing Masses as often as they can find them. Many people have many beautiful stories associated with a miraculous healing from the event.

Jen sat next to me and her mother by her side. We attended the Mass and many of my friends and customers also came as well. The Mass started and Father Albert, invited everyone up to the altar to receive a blessing after the Mass. I went up with my friend Ann Marie and we both fell back. We were on the hard floor without feeling it whatsoever. It was a very beautiful experience of peace. When I awoke I had no pain of the floor or felt I was even on the floor. I went back to my seat and saw Jen crying. She felt because she did not fall back she did not receive a healing. I assured her that was not the way it worked and I would continue to pray for her in Adoration.

I asked Jen what she did for work in the past and she said she was a speech pathologist for children. I was happy to hear this and asked her if she could help me. She didn't know I had a stutter and told me I should say what I wanted to say in a public speaking event regardless of the stutter which she felt was not noticeable at all. She couldn't help me because her speciality is with children. She said she would pray for me to have the courage to speak and not to be afraid.

I asked Jen if she could go to Wakefield Adoration Chapel and she told me she knew Father Ron at that church, and he had also been praying for her as well. She did not know Adoration was offered there and I suggested she attend and offer her cancer to Jesus in prayer. I decided I would focus praying for her full time and Ann Marie and I sent her flowers for Mothers Day. She continued to pray and told me in an email her tumor was slowly shrinking and she had more time.

It was May and my friends wanted to throw me a birthday party. I did not want to celebrate my birthday this year. I wanted to go to Divine Mercy in Stockbridge for the day and offer my day for Jen. Besides, I thought to myself "why should I celebrate another year when so many want to live for another year". My birthday came and I went alone to Stockbridge. I drove up there and offered my whole day of prayer for Jen.

I had a wonderful time and knew I was going for the sole purpose to offer everything for Jen. I prayed through Mary and to Sister Faustina and to God. I told him about her twin daughters and her wanting to get better. She wanted to see her daughters get married. When I came home I felt I had done the right thing by offering my day to another soul and I felt certain this time God would hear my prayers. I reached out to Jen a few months later and she was going to Adoration and feeling better. She also got the go ahead from her doctor to go back to work in the fall of 2014. Her doctors thought it would be good for her positive outlook and her tumor was shrinking.

My parish, Saint Williams, in Tewksbury was looking for someone to help with the landscaping and I offered along with my mom to help. My mother was 83 at the time and I thought she would like to plant some flowers out front for the church. I bought Father Andrew Knopp, OMI, a solar fountain of Saint Francis and he was so excited. He placed it near the side entrance of the Rectory. I had purchased one for my townhouse as well. It was very beautiful and went on and off by itself. I also bought all the flowers and my mom and I devoted a few hours one evening to plant.

It was July of 2014, and I wanted to go to Montreal with my son. Keep in mind I had never been and I wanted to visit Saint Joseph's shrine. It was Saint Andre Bessette who I had seen in the Eucharist in 2010, and I did not know too much about this shrine. We made plans to go for a week. I searched around the internet for a place to stay and the Oratory onsite happened to have two rooms available. It is right next to the shrine and I thought how beautiful this will be to experience staying here. When we arrived after a 6 hour drive, I immediately wanted to visit the Shrine. We walked in and went to the chapel. My son and I sat in the chapel for about an hour. It was so beautiful and peaceful. He was admiring the building since he was in college for Mechanical Engineering.

UNITY FOR ALL

I went to the tomb and draped myself over it praying for peace amongst my family members. I prayed we would find our way back together even despite all we have been through. The next day while in my room on my iPad I heard in a whisper, "**The battle is over**". It was in a man's whisper. This was very interesting to hear and I attributed it to what had been happening with my family.

Maybe God heard my prayers and a peaceful resolution was on its way. I also told the people who worked there how I saw Brother Andre in the Eucharist in 2010, prior to him being canonized. We were there for five days and then came home. It was a very beautiful experience and I encourage all to visit.

My son also went back with his girlfriend two weeks later and they had a very good time. He took her to see the beautiful Church and they visited the shrine.

When I came back from Montreal the next day I went to Mass at Saint Mary's in Lawrence. When they carried the gifts up to the altar I looked at the communion and I saw a white spirit all around the communion. I noticed this from the time they passed me right up to the altar. I never saw that before. I also felt a deep deep deep love come over me and this joy was from my heart. I was in love a million times more than before. I enjoyed this happy and joyful event. I knew something was much different than last time. I was experiencing a pure joy at the Mass or when the priest mentioned God or Jesus I felt complete joy and could not stop smiling. I was forever different as this is still happening today. If anyone mentions the name Jesus or God around me, take a look at my face. I suppose it's similar when someone mentions something to you that you absolutely love to hear and this is what happens to me.

I was invited by Muriel Neveux to attend "Life in the Spirit" for five weeks in Methuen, Ma. I never even heard of this before but elected to go. Father Albert thought it would be good for me to get into this group and they could help me with my brokenness to speak. I did attend and each week a speaker got up and talked a little about their journey. I knew they wanted others to contribute something but we all felt comfortable talking in our little groups of eight people. I met some wonderful friends at this meeting.

I enjoyed it thoroughly. I remember them telling me it was mandatory I attend a session close to the end because Father Martin had to pray over all of us to release the gifts of the Holy Spirit. As we formed a circle and our sponsors prayed behind us I was sitting in a chair praying in tongues and all I could see was a white light in front of me during this forty five minute session. I was on fire and sweating from head to toe. My friends could not touch me as they could feel this heat radiating. As Father Martin got closer to me he knew what God wanted him to say. He began to tell me I would be travelling world wide for Jesus.

I could hear Muriel telling him I have a stammer and he doused my mouth with Holy oil and prayed in tongues.

As he did this, I became even more fluent in my speech and as he walked past me I felt a great Peace come over me. I was asking Him to take this burden from me and allow me to do His work. I kept reciting, "Jesus I trust in You". "Jesus, I trust in You", "Jesus, I trust in You". It was quite beautiful. There was another meeting the following week and they were looking for a volunteer to speak. I purposely did not come for fear I would be asked. I found out they did want me to speak at that event.

I went to a healing service offered by Father Diorio in Sturbridge. I had heard about him and wanted to experience his gifts. Father Diorio who is an Italian priest with gifts of healing, prophercy and knowledge. He is world renowned. I wrote to him on the computer first and let him know I would be coming to one of his events. I went on to tell him I had a stutter and asked if there was a special prayer to get rid of it. I was desperate for a healing of this which I felt was holding me back for years.

I went to his service and fell right back at the altar. As I went down I heard the words, "Miracle Healer" over and over again. I was slain in the spirit for at least 10 minutes.

I woke up and felt great! Another time I went again and I sat next to two women and the woman on my left introduced herself as Ginny, from Chelmsford. She had an issue with her heart and was very uncomfortable sitting in her chair. I asked her if she heard about Adoration and she didn't, but she was Catholic. I told her about the Perpetual Adoration Chapel in Lawrence and in Tewksbury. She told me she was originally from Lawrence.

She was from that area and lived two blocks from Saint Mary's. She had no idea about Adoration and I proceeded to tell her how beautiful it is to sit in His presence. I then offered them a ride home. They accepted and called their family member not to pick them up since I lived nearby and would be taking them home. We stopped at Saint Mary's, in Lawrence, on the way home and I introduced them to Father John who happened to be outside and in front of the chapel when we arrived. Ginny really liked Adoration and was happy to know it was available 24/7.

I took Ginny home and met her Fiance. I left them my ministry card and told them I looked forward to seeing them at a healing Mass in the future with Father Albert.

I then called Father Diorio soon afterwards and left a voicemail about helping me with my stutter. He had his secretary call me back and she told me I had to go into the woods with my van and scream as loud as I could for fifteen minutes. I had to ask Jesus to take this stuttering from me. I didn't feel comfortable doing it. I knew if anyone heard me screaming and I was alone I was afraid I would be spotted. There was no way I was about to go into the dark woods with my van and start screaming. No possible way. I asked for another solution. She did not offer one.

Father Albert was coming back from vacation and asked me if I wanted to join him to the Madonna House in Combermere, Canada. I was never there and he gave me her books. I loved reading the Poustinia, written by Catherine Doherty. You can read more about this beautiful place at www.madonnahouse.org. He went many times and thought I would enjoy it. We would drive up and I offered to make a donation of office supplies, and he brought items that he had for many years as donations. It was approximately 508 miles. The ride seemed easy and we talked and listened to Holy music all the way there. When we arrived at night I stayed in the girls house and he stayed in the Priest house up the street. The ride up was about 11 hours and I drove most of it. I love to drive and enjoyed it very much. I felt very comfortable there and they made me feel like I was part of their family. If you like rustic you will fit in nicely.

Madonna House has Adoration of the Blessed Sacrament for four hours a day and their nearby Parish Church has Adoration of the Blessed Sacrament Monday through Friday 24/7. We met at Mass each morning and we walked to Mass. It was different and I encourage everyone to visit the Madonna House to experience a beautiful community of people all working together. The singing I enjoyed every morning as well as meeting people from all over the world who live there and work there.

The food is very very good and all home made from scratch. I continued to talk of Adoration to each and every person I met. They seemed to like Adoration as well. I will never forget my first night there when the lights went out I felt the presence of Mary right at the foot of my bed.

This was such a welcoming feeling. I travelled to the Madonna House two times in one year and each time bringing them donations of office supplies since this is what I did for a living it seemed fitting since they needed so much. Father Albert brought them donations too.

UNITY FOR ALL

When we were coming back home Father Albert suggested we pull off to the side of the road. I asked him why we had stopped here and he told me do what Father Diorio wanted me to do. It was raining outside and wet. He insisted I do it because the moment was there and he thought since we were together he could stay in my van and I could walk ahead where he could still see me. I did as he suggested. I walked out and found an area in the fields to start screaming. As I was screaming in the rain I noticed it stopped raining. I looked up into the sky and started screaming as loud as I could, "Jesus, Do you hear me? How can I do your work if you left me with a fear of Public Speaking and a Stutter? Please take this from Me. If you take this from me I can be your voice". Please take this from me I shouted AND SHOUTED AND SHOUTED. I asked OVER AND OVER AGAIN. PLEASE TAKE THIS STUTTER FROM ME SO I CAN DO YOUR HOLY WORK".

The rain stopped and the sun was shining on my face. I decided to walk back to my van. As I approached my van I saw Father Albert. I got into my van and he said. That was good but you were only out there for ten minutes. We will have to do it again for fifteen. My thoughts where, "Father Albert, Are you serious?".

It was November of 2014, and I felt the strong desire to travel to Saint Joseph Shrine after Thanksgiving, in Montreal, Canada. My friends all thought I should go with someone or not go at all. All I knew was I had to go and I must plan now. I called the Oratory and they happen to have one room available for that weekend. I booked it. As the day approached right after Thanksgiving I knew that next morning I was going to Montreal, Canada. It was five days prior and a deer hit the side of my van and sent me out across the street in the middle of a road. I almost hit a pole. I pulled my van over and I was shaken up a bit. My door was hit and dented. I wasn't going to let a little dent stop me from travelling.

UNITY FOR ALL

I knew I had to go no matter what and it was a strong feeling. The day came and I left at 5:00 AM in the morning. I was very excited and looking forward to it. I took my laptop to work on my diary and I knew Jesus would be there and I were to spend my time in Adoration. The drive up was approximately 308 miles and I would pray on my way up and listen to Holy music. I was very excited as I passed Vermont and was in Canada.

When I arrived I checked in to the Oratory immediately and drove myself to the chapel to pray. I was excited about being there and went to the tomb and to the store and just enjoyed my visit.

I then went back to my room and ate a salad for dinner. I went to sleep and woke up the next day. I worked on my diary and went to the Oratory in the early afternoon.

What surprised me was when I got to the Adoration Chapel there was no soul around. I was alone with Jesus. I apologized to him and sat there and promised him I would not leave until another soul arrived. I knew this offends Jesus to be alone. There was a Mass on the other side but, it was in French and I could not understand one word they said. All I knew was he was alone and I was there to be with him.

I prayed with him and went into a deep meditation. I stayed with Jesus for many more hours alone. He told me he was not happy that souls were spending time with the saints and not with Him. He expressed priests spending one Holy Hour a day in front of the Blessed Sacrament and this being mandatory. He told me if the priests spend one hour a day they would love him and there would be no more sin from the priests.

He also told me to get that message out there. I told him I would, but I really did not know how I was going to get it out since I can not do Public Speaking. I kept hearing "One God – True God – One God – True God". Jesus wants to get out of the tabernacle and on the altars around the world. He was clear on the Message. I knew what he was asking of me, but I was not the one to do it. I kept telling him I am the mouse my father had called me since I was a child. He picked the wrong person. I am

UNITY FOR ALL

weak in speech. Here I am age 54, and still had a fear to speak. He said the priests must open the Chapels and take the hour and then souls will follow. I now knew my fate. I knew I had to make this happen. He said you will be saved and do as I ask of you. As soon as he said this, people started coming in. I then saw about ten people in Adoration at the shrine.

I then went around to the church and saw hundreds of people in the shrine for the Mass. I asked the security guard what was going on and he said a retreat for the people and I can go in if I sit in the back. I did. I sat in the back and participated in the Mass. I even went up for Communion even though I did not understand one word the priest had said. The Mass was in French and I did not speak French, even though I am half French. I still stayed and when the Mass was over I started to venture out to the back, and then I noticed the Bishop from the back came out. I did not know he was there prior. I wanted to meet him in person and waited. I had to wait in line and then asked another priest if I could say hello to him. When the Bishop was free I was offered a chance to say hello. I walked up to him and he asked me my name. I told him I am Suzanne from Massachusetts and Jesus sent me here for a few days. I told him all about the Ministry and Adoration is Unity for All. He told me his sermon was based on Adoration and his name was "Bishop Christian Lepene" for Montreal. I told him I did not speak French and I was just in Adoration and Jesus was all alone.

I also suggested he read my story and that Our Blessed Mother wants Adoration as "Unity" for all souls. I could have spoken to him all day and I only had five minutes. I handed him my ministry card and was on my way back to the Oratory. I felt in my heart I was sent there to hand him the Ministry card and tell him Adoration is Unity for All. I was so convinced that was why I was called to Montreal. Little did I know there was more to come.

The next morning I was going home. I felt well rested and went out to my van and put my suitcase in the back and sat in the front seat. I was so glad to be going home and it was bright, sunny and early. I figure if I left at 8:00 AM I would be home by 2:00 pm.

This would give me plenty of time to get ready for work the next day and unpack. When I was about to leave I realized I did not give my friend at the desk one of my mini tea lights. I wanted to go back and give this to him. I put my pocketbook under my passenger seat. I then proceeded to go in and met the receptionist at the desk. She invited me for a free breakfast but I insisted I had to go back. I told her I left my pocketbook under the seat and she assured me she would watch my van. I remembered they have signs that say "under survellience" as well. I thought "Maybe I should go eat before I go". I just had my keys on me and proceeded up the stairs and made breakfast.

I was watching my van and eating and then a couple came over whom I was talking with about Adoration. It was a doctor who was visiting the area and I gave them my ministry card and told him the blessings of Adoration and how there is one right in the shrine. I then left after about 30 minutes speaking with him. I went downstairs and said bye to the woman at the front desk. When I walked out to my van, which was at about the same time as the doctor, I had no idea what was about to happen. I opened my door and to my surprise there was glass all over my front seat. I was screaming and scared out of my wits. I did not know yet what had happened. I thought at first they smashed my glass roof but I realized they smashed my passenger window and stole my pocketbook. I was in shock and I was screaming. I have been robbed! I have been robbed!!!

I ran inside the Oratory and told the woman what had happened to me. I asked her if she did watch my van and she said she did but a call came in. How can this happen? Can you check the cameras and she told me they do not work, the signs were fake. The cameras broke years ago and they have them there to scare the robbers.

I was all alone and robbed. I only had my car keys. I went back to my van and in horror I had glass all over the place and I found my iPad in the back which had a crack in it but it worked. I also found my diary which I took out the night prior and my passport I took out as well. I brought these things back into the Oratory and went on Facebook and told my friends I was robbed. I was scared out of my wits. I started praying and a deep deep peace came over me. Jesus was protecting me. I felt very calm after this and I settled down 100% percent. I was no longer frightened and I had to trust in GOD to get home.

The calls came in. First Father Albert was able to call me and it took him awhile. He was In California and suggested I talk with the priest to see if they would loan me money for gas and I could wire it from home. I called the Shrine and no priest could help me get home. I was so sad. I then called my banks and asked if they could wire me the money. My bank came through and said they could but the Oratory did not have the money in the draw to help me get home. I felt doomed. I then spoke with my son and he said if no one could help me he would come from home and help me. I am sure my friends at home were now wishing I stayed home but, I had no regrets even at this point of why I had to go there. I knew I had to trust and GOD would help me. About twenty minutes later a man came out of the back of the room and said he would help me. He was from Morocco and he heard my conversation and he said he could take me to the police station in my van which I would drive and make a statement.

We drove there and I was not scared and when we arrived I went inside and made a statement. He told me he was robbed as well about two weeks prior and the robbers stole his passport. He searched the grounds and found another bag but it was not mine.

UNITY FOR ALL

I learned that people watch you from above and when they see people put their pocketbooks under their seat they wait and steal it. It happens there and also at the shrine. I was all alone and he knew I wanted to get home. The woman at the Oratory thought I should stay a few more days and it was not my time to go home and maybe the Lord wanted me to stay. I felt I should go home and I could not leave my van in the parking lot with a smashed window. I had to get home and go to work the very next day. I was doomed. We then drove to Walmart and bought tape and he told me he would give me $100.00, US Currency, to get home. I was so happy. He handed me $100.00, Canada money and taped up my window and I went inside and called my son and told him I was coming home. When I came out of the Oratory and walked to my vehicle he told me he felt my joy which was radiating all around me and he knew I wanted to be with my son and get out of there. I was happy he did all this work for me and I was on my way home. He insisted I go in the building and make my phone calls and get ready to go home. I came out and my van was all taped up and ready to go. It was around 3:00 PM, and I was ready for home.

I hugged him and thanked him and he told me he was going to go to the Chapel once he had the time. He told me he was muslim and stayed at the Oratory many times and never went to Adoration once in his life. I told him Adoration is "Unity for All" and all souls are invited to go to Adoration. I assured him he would find Peace and Love with God. I got in my van and drove off.

I was going home. As I drove a few miles away from Montreal a dark cloud appeared over my van and my navigational system turned off. I could not believe it. I was lost as I can not read a map and I did not have a cell phone. How can I get home if I do not know which direction to even take? I pulled over and turned my van off. I turned it back on again. I almost started crying. I turned my van on and off and on the 3rd time I prayed to GOD to help me. I said, "GOD please help me I want to go home, Jesus I trust in you!".

UNITY FOR ALL

My car started and my navigational turned on. I drove to the border and stopped for a loaf of bread and found an additional $35.00 in a compartment in my van. I did not know I had it and there it was $35.00 in USA Money. I used that to buy my loaf of wheat bread and some juice and drove right through Montreal and into Vermont. I was coming home. I stopped for gas and never had to use the 100.00.

It was my security and I was coming home. I was dancing in my seat all the way home singing praises to GOD. I finally got home at 11:00 PM due to traffic and weather and my window even all taped up was fine. I was happy to be home and when I came through the front door my son was right there. We talked for two hours over the incident. I went to bed and off to work the next day.

We were now in December of 2014, and I began to go to Adoration more and more and explained to Jesus I did not know how to get the message out to the priests about spending an hour a day in Adoration. I know my Pastor was in Adoration all the time but, I did not know how much other Pastors did it at their parishes. I told Geri what had happened to me and she told me I am in the Interior Castle!

In my bedroom on December 5th I heard, **"You must do Gods work and blessings will be bestowed on you and your family forever"**. I then thought about what He said over and over again and said, "Jesus I can only help soul by soul". I work full time and I have a son in college full time. The ministry is my devotion in bringing souls to You one on one. I am comfortable with this life now.

I went into a great peace in my bedroom and I recited over and over.

Jesus is my **Joy – Joy - Joy**

Jesus is my **Spouse – Spouse – Spouse**

UNITY FOR ALL

Jesus is my **Life – Life – Life**

Jesus is my **Peace – Peace – Peace**

I wish the world to know You as I do and feel you inside as I do. If more souls knew the blessings of Adoration this world would be of Peace. I am blessed because of You. I love You

Jesus. I do love you. I do not know how I can leave my job and go out and speak of You to the crowds. Please show me "how I am to do this."

Soon it was December 6th and this was my mother's birthday. I went to her house and she was not there. I wanted to take her out to eat. I decided I would go back later. When I arrived I met a nurse. She told me my mother had fallen at the restaurant and needed to go in the hospital but she refused. The nurse was asking my mother all sorts of questions and she could not answer them. I realized at this point my mom's memory was much worse than I had earlier thought.

She did not know what year it was, who was the president and she even had her address in her mind of the large house she lived at five years prior. We made plans that for Christmas she was coming with me to my house. She wanted this very much. I checked on her the next few days and noticed she could barely walk but she again refused to go to the hospital.

On Christmas Day I was about to pick her up and I received the dreaded call. My brother Peter immediately phoned me to tell me that our mother was in the hospital. I told my son we were to go there and spend the day with her. We both went down and she was in the emergency room.

She had cracked her pelvic bone area when she had fallen and it was much worse. She was to stay there until they could find a rehab for her. My brother Peter told me he doubted she could ever go back considering she had no idea how to cook and take care of herself anymore.

As it turned out after they did more tests on her they told us she had Dementia. It meant we had to find a place for her and my brother visited two Assisted Living with Memory care and he chose Bayberry in Tewksbury. Mom could not go there first she had to go to another place in Chelmsford. She liked it there very much but they did not offer the care she needed for her memory. It was 2015, and she was going to live in Bayberry, now called Avita for Dementia. It was very close to my home and I knew I was going to be there for her as much as she needed me.

Chapter Six

The time had come to take all of my mother's paintings down and move them to her new place. My mother was an accomplished artist of over 50 years, winning many ribbons in categories such as oil and watercolors. She chose the paintings she wanted to keep and allowed us to go to her townhouse to select the paintings each of us wanted. I already had fifteen of her best paintings, including some portraits, but nevertheless, I went back to choose a few more. I asked mother for permission to gift one of her watercolors to Father Albert for Saint Mary's Church. He displayed it in the hall, in the rectory. It was a spectacular watercolor of various teapots. Mother had done an exceptionally beautiful job painting this one approximately ten years earlier. All of her paintings stayed in the family with the exception of the one we that we gifted to Father Albert.

As far as the rest of mother's belongs, my sister opted to keep her bed and sofa. We slowly and methodically went through many other items together as well. Mother had already let me know that she wanted me to have her fine china which meant a lot to her. Given how nostalgic this china set was for all of us, I decided to share the set with my sister. One room at a time, we went through and sorted various items. We were informed that everything left in the garage must be sorted and removed, otherwise, it would automatically be donated.

I decided to spend the day in the garage sorting through everything, choosing what to keep for myself and what would be donated to charity. It was March in 2015, as I sorted through her garage when I saw this beautiful, ornate silverware chest peeking out behind piles of other items. Despite how ancient and dusty it looked, I could tell it had character.

Carefully, I removed it from the pile and managed to bring it into her townhouse despite the fact that it was so heavy. After carefully opening and closing the various drawers and compartments, I decided I would definitely bring it back home with me. Now I had this gorgeous chest that need just a little tender loving care in addition to my mom's and her mom's crystal. I also received china their china and silverware from 1800's. This was a silverplated silverware set. I absolutely loved the pattern, desperately wishing that I could identify the year and name of the pattern. I was incredibly excited that these would be handed down to me and honestly, quite surprised that none of my siblings wanted this set. As I turned it over to look at the pattern, I couldn't believe my eyes I thought to myself, "This must be a mistake. How can this pattern be called **"Adoration?"** Immediately, I snapped a picture of it with my cell phone enlarging it so I could take a closer look. Needless to say, I was shocked!

I sat in her kitchen for at least 15 minutes just pondering this. Now, more than ever, I knew this was meant to be. This was my path. Deep in my heart, I knew that God was trying to get my attention and He had it. I immediately posted that picture online to share it with my family. I then rushed to see my mother who told me how her mother had given her the set when she married but never actually used it. It was mine to cherish and mine to use. That following Easter, instead of going out for our traditional meal I used that set. I never went out to dinner for Easter again. I stay in every year and use it. I was convinced that God planned all of this from the day I was born. **Psalm 139:16**

All my previous thoughts no longer mattered. This was my call and His mission. I was completely in with the Lord. I surrendered and went to the altar and said, YES.

Yes, I will follow you and Yes, I will do your Holy will. I realized any one of my siblings could have picked up that set of silverware. It was meant for me. I started to think of all the things that could have happened to that set since my mom had it for over 50 years and it just sat in her home with no usage. It followed her from home to home never being used. My grandmother gave it to her in the 50's and my mom kept it but did not use it. God knew before I was born that I was meant for this mission.

UNITY FOR ALL

I found myself talking once again of Adoration to everyone in the Assisted Living Residence. I bought them medals and the elderly loved them. At Bayberry there are people who are retired and wish to live there. There are also people who need help and have memory issues. I would check in at least three times a week, and on the weekends spend a whole day with her by taking her to the ocean. She got so used to praying with me and coming to Adoration she liked her time with me. As long as we were together she would go anywhere and do anything. One time we went to five Adoration Chapels in one day. I thought this was wonderful, she only complained once. Jesus was healing us both and the time with her was priceless. She was 84 years old and told me as long as she was with me she would gladly go and sit. She even admitted the peace was helping her with so many issues she had been dealing with.

I know that she missed her cat very much when she did not go back to her townhouse, but she had less responsibilities and I was always taking her out.

My brother was also living in Tewksbury at the time and would take care of her medication for the first year before I took it over. We felt since I was always there and taking her out it would be more efficient if I was her sole first response. My brother being a builder was not always building close by and he had lots of meetings. I worked just 40 hours a week and I could take off from work whenever an emergency came up.

I met a woman name Jennifer who happened to work at Bayberry and knew my family. She started telling me she had not been to Church in over twenty years. I brought up Adoration to her but the time was an issue. She then reached out to me about her mom having a heart attack and being intensive care as well as her grandmother having heart issues.

I asked her if she would meet me in Adoration in Tewksbury, she did. She met me one night at 9:00 PM. She found it very peaceful. She prayed and let me pray with her. Her grandmother was in her 90's and passed away, but her mom survived. She has met me there again, and has also started going back to Church. She signed up to be a Eucharist minister at her Church in Lowell, and her faith is on track.

I was also starting to interview for a new job. I really wanted to get back to engineering sales which I had done in the past. I was looking for an inside sales position. I applied at a few companies, but everyone wanted to hire me for outside sales. I wanted to be a part of the team and work in an office daily. I needed the health care and the steady income that was offered at my current position. I started to interview and found myself talking about Adoration while on the Interview.

The Holy Spirit came upon me at each and every interview. I found myself arguing with the Holy Spirit and telling Him before I went in for the interview that I was not to bring up Adoration. I have to tell you as I sit here and write this, He had different plans. He was calling these souls back to Him and I was His messenger. One day out of the blue while on the road I received a call from an agency. This woman was the President and CEO of a staffing firm, and she wanted to meet with me. She agreed to meet me off site so that we could talk. I did not want to go into that field, but I agreed to meet with her. If she had a position for me, that would be wonderful.

I remember walking in and there she was. She wanted to hire me as a business partner and was very open about it. I told her I did not want to do that type of work since I felt it may be difficult sale with all the free job boards in the industry as well as the competition on each block.

I expressed my desire to work as inside sales and full time. As I sat there and answered all her questions in the restaurant I felt the presence of the Holy Spirit come upon me. I knew at that point, it was 'His' appointment, and not mine. I asked her what denomination she was and she told me Catholic, she was taken back by my question. She then told me she felt my presence was soothing to her soul and I told her it was GOD. She then said it had been a long time since she had gone to church.

UNITY FOR ALL

I sat there and let her speak for at least fifteen minutes. I refused to say one word. She told me as a child her grandmother used to make her do time out in the corner and recite a rosary. She went to a Catholic school and college as well. She also met her Catholic husband. It was a very beautiful story she was sharing with me. She also told me that her daughter recently asked her to let her go to confirmation classes.

She did not want to go back to the Catholic Church and told her daughter no. I proceeded to talk with her about Adoration. She thought that was only around Easter. I told her that the church in her town had Adoration on certain days. She looked at me, convinced God sent me to her. She had Him on her mind for a while. She then broke down and cried right in the restaurant. I did not know what I said or did but she said, I have a secret to tell you. Can you help me? I assured her I would try. She told me she was battling cancer and it was getting worse. I told her she can win this. She needed to surrender and I held her hand and prayed with her. I noticed that people in the restaurant were staring at us. I didn't care. I needed to help her and this time I needed the Lord's help. I cried out to the Holy Spirit in the middle of the restaurant for the grace to heal her in this fight against cancer. She was crying so much and did not want to suffer anymore. I told her we were going to give it to the Lord. She went into a great peace right at the restaurant. She told me she felt very good and stopped crying. We hugged and talked more about Adoration. I even asked her if she wanted some Holy oil which I had in my van at the time. I wanted her to ask our Blessed Mother to intervene for her because she was close to her rosary beads. I told her to say, "Mary, Take Over" when she felt powerless. Those are powerful words even in the business world. I knew if anyone could help her it would be our Blessed Mother. I put all of this in God's Hands.

As we drank our tea and spoke for another hour I also knew she would beat this cancer. She followed me out to my car while it was pouring rain. I anointed her with Holy oil and gave her the ministry card. I asked that we stay in touch and I would refer people to her if she promised me should would recite a rosary and thank our Blessed Mother for helping her. She called me a few days later to tell me she won an account by asking "Mary take over" just when she thought she had lost the account.

I received another call for an interview. I was hesitant since I knew the Holy Spirit was going to lead me to another soul. A few days go by and I decide to call them back and go on the interview. I set it up on a vacation day and while in my van I prayed and asked the Lord to please leave me alone. I really wanted a new job. I wanted something for me and I felt this could be the company. I told God this time I was not going to discuss Adoration and I really was going to fight with it all the way. I proceeded to walk in the company and filled out the paperwork. It seemed like a larger company and I could fit in well there. They had me go into the conference room and wait for the Director. I sat at the very end of a 30' conference table. I was admiring the table which was a cream color and not brown like most conference tables. The chairs were very fancy in cream as well and they had about 30 of them to match the beautiful table. As I sat there I felt very comfortable and within twenty minutes I was introduced to the Director of Sales from the Director of Human Resources. She said, "Suzanne I would like for you to meet the Director you may be working with". I shook his hand and sat down. He sat to my left and I stayed at the end of the table as if I was the leader. I felt as if I was leading him and he was not leading the interview.

He asked me many questions and I answered all of them. I felt this great peace come upon me as I spoke and realized I was very calm in this interview and spoke very well. He wanted me to tell him why he should buy office supplies from me versus the vendor he currently uses. I gave him a great story which he felt he never thought about prior. He asked me what I wanted for vacation time and told me about the pay structure.

He then proceeded with one last question. He wanted to know what "**was my biggest obstacle in life**". I told him Public Speaking. He asked me why.

I then proceeded to tell him that I had a ministry and I felt if I could speak in front of people I could do the will of God, but because I had a fear of Public Speaking, I was not 100% ready to do His will. I also told him all about Adoration. He told me that he is from Lawrence, and has his grandmothers rosary. He also told me he used to love to go to church and since his grandmother had passed away he stopped attending. He loved the Holy Rosary church very much and often drove by it with a tear in his eye. He did not know that Saint Mary's had Adoration, but stated that he needed peace in his life. He also told me he was a Public Speaker at College and he said this was the biggest obstacle in people's lives which is why he teaches this class for over twenty years. He said you need to find something that is your passion and then you will love to talk about it. I told him Adoration is my passion and my life and I could not stop talking about God and all the wonderful things He can do for our souls. I then realized after thirty minutes that God planned this interview as well. I looked at him and asked him if I had the job. He said No. He said not until you do God's will.

He didn't think he could get my attention. He felt I had another job much more important and I needed to try public speaking. I needed to try and do it just once. He said if you try it and you do not like it then come back and re-apply. As we walked to the door I shook his hand and I said, God always wins.

I decided I was not going to interview for a while. I needed to focus on the ministry and continue to bring people to Adoration. I was so busy after work meeting people in Wakefield, Lawrence as well as in Tewksbury. Everywhere I went, even at restaurants I could not stop spreading the Word.

One day while in line at a Chinese restaurant I could hear the woman behind me talk about her job and how unhappy she was there.

I told her about Adoration and she said she was Catholic. She had never heard of Adoration. I told her to read my story online and gave her the address to Saint Williams. She told me her name was Jean and she had a lot of stress from a company she was no longer with. I shook her hand and was on my way to church. She phoned me a few days later to tell me her story. She went to Adoration and sat there and prayed to God.

When she got out of Adoration she got a call from a lawyer whom told her he would not take her case. He had second thoughts and decided to take her case. It was an answer to her prayer is what she told me.

One day my coworker came into my office and asked me if I could pray for her father-in-law. His name was Harry and he was in his 80s and was diabetic. He needed heart surgery and she was afraid he was not going to make it. Her husband was also working with us as a driver and she was worried for him and his sister who also lived with her. I told her I would pray for him and asked if Jesus healed him would she come to Adoration and thank him? She said she would. She has not been to a Catholic Church in a very long time. I went to Adoration that very same night and I prayed for her father-in-law. He went for the surgery on his heart and did so well when he came out of it they released him the next day. I met her at Adoration and met Helen, her sister in-law. They liked it very much and Helen went back a few other times and felt so much peace. I gave her a set of rosary beads which I had with me at the time. They meant a lot to me, but I felt she should have them. I did have an extra set at home of the same type. I was happy Adoration gave her the peace she needed in her life.

A few months went by when I received a call from a woman. She grew up in Tewksbury and knew my older sisters. I did not know her because of our age difference, however, my sister did and my younger brother is also friends with her brother. She called me to tell me about my aunt who had been diagnosed recently with cancer. She did not tell any of us and she wanted to know if I could invite my Aunt to Adoration. We talked about it but without confronting her about knowing she had pancreatic cancer, how would we convince her to come?

I asked her what denomination she was and she said, "Born Again". I asked her if she wanted to come to Adoration and she refused. She told me she was not Catholic. I told her Adoration is "Unity For All". She would not budge. We decided we would speak again. She called me two months later to tell me she was

UNITY FOR ALL

in so much pain and needed to know if I would pray with her over the phone. I asked her if she would like to join me at Adoration. I began to tell her how much Jesus could help her. She agreed to meet me there. It was late at night and I wanted to go and help her. I felt if she was in this much pain the very least I could do was come and help her.

I arrived and did not know what to expect, as I said I did not know her and did not know what she looked like. When I arrived just one other fellow was in the Chapel so we found each other quickly. I did not know she had a rolling walker and metal crutches. She was very nice and told me she had pain over her entire body. I asked her to sit next to me but, she told me she cannot sit in the chair. She was injured as a Peace Corp volunteer. She had a blanket and she put it on the floor which was vinyl and layed on it. I told her to look at Jesus and I would pray over her while she gave all this pain to Jesus.

I then prayed to Jesus, I said, "Jesus, if you truly want this ministry to be 'Unity for All' please heal her, please take away all her pain and fill her body with your Peace."

I prayed this over and over "Lord, Show me a miracle. Please heal her". She stayed only for 20 minutes. She then got up and carried her rolling walker and crutches up the stairs. She did not take the elevator. She said she did not need any help. She was on her way home. I then left a few hours after and the next day she woke up with the greatest joy and peace she ever felt in her life. She went around the whole town saying, "Unity for All", she had been healed.

I had to explain to her that Jesus is in the Eucharist and He healed her. It was His way of letting her know that He is the healer and He is here for us. She continues to visit our beautiful Adoration Chapel. My aunt was also healed of Pancreatic Cancer. Jesus was healing everyone! Jesus I trust in You!!!

A few months pass and I met **Monsignor Donato Conte** from the Vatican. He has visited the Boston area for many years. He visits Medford, Ma. every late summer and stays until October and he especially likes St. Joseph's in Wakefield. I met him there

UNITY FOR ALL

at praise and worship, on a Monday evening. I introduced myself to him and gave him my ministry tri-fold. He told me he knew a Bob DeCarolis from Italy when he was a young child and asked me if we were related, I did not know at that time. I have relatives in Italy, but I do not know all of them nor have I ever gone, but my parents and relatives have many times. What I did not realize was Monsignor was also a Mystic and he told me within two weeks that I am here for a mission. I expressed my fear of public speaking, but he assured me on God's time. I spent two summers with him. He would call me when he came to the area and gave me his residence number in Italy.

I often took my mother to his Sunday Mass at Saint Anthony's Catholic Church in Everett,. He told me to come to the 10:30 am Mass. It was an italian Mass, and we enjoyed it even though we both did not speak italian.

He also invited me to come to Italy and to stay at the apartments at the Vatican. He would take me to the Adoration Chapels. He started to call me to take him to praise and worship weekly at Wakefield. I enjoyed doing this as he had words for me every time I picked him up. He even came one day to Saint Mary's in Lawrence. We went to Adoration for an hour together. It was so beautiful. As I sat there with him praying I felt a strong presence. We also went to a healing Mass with Father Albert in Methuen, Ma. Father was very polite in introducing him to the congregation and Monsignor loved to talk about Saint Padre Pio. He had his vestment which was given to him years ago. He wanted so badly to write my book and print it from the Vatican. He came back in 2016, and we spent a few hours together before his trip back to the Vatican. He kept telling me I need to have the courage to speak and spread the message on Adoration.

He promised me when he came back in 2017, and he did say "God willing" since he had some heart trouble, that we would visit some churches in New England area together. I knew if he was with me and did most of the talking I would participate. Sadly, Monsignor Donato Conte passed away Feb 21, 2017. I made a video of him while he was in my office at my new position and will treasure it and his words to me as long as I live. He also shared with me some pictures of a book he wanted to publish when he went back to the Vatican. He allowed me to keep a copy of the pictures which he cut out and took the others to send back to the Vatican.

Suzanne DeCarolis, Msgr Donato Conte, Mike Spinelli

I began to pray deeply with our Lord. He tells me that I need to talk to the Catholic channels about having a show based on Adoration alone. I wrote to many of them, the response was they do not have a spot for it. I then went back to the altar and told Jesus that I had not heard back. He told me I need to do it, I told him I have a fear of speaking. He assured me I need to do it. I decided to go to the Monastery in N. Guilford, CT. I spoke to the Superior that I was there seeking guidance from God.

I love spending time at the garden which is across the street. The peaceful surrounding is delightful for my soul. I immediately feel our Lady's presence while sitting there. As I sat there praying for God's will within five minutes two women came into the garden. They came over to me and asked me if I was from the area. I told them I was from Massachusetts, and seeking direction from God. I also told them I have a love of Adoration. They asked me about Adoration. I asked them if they were Catholic. They are Catholic and never heard of Adoration. They told me they are from Connecticut and have been shopping at the Catholic store in Our Lady of Grace Monastery for over nine years. I told them in that church is Perpetual Adoration! They never knew, nor went. I asked them how much time they had. They told me just eight minutes and came to do the stations of the cross. I invited them to Adoration. I started to get this great big JOY come over me and I knew this was what GOD wanted me to do. He wanted me to invite them over and then take a video of them for the new website. As we walked over to the chapel I had the greatest JOY in my Soul. I was on FIRE. I felt so happy and joyful, words cannot even describe. I opened the door and inside we went. We sat down and I watched them kiss the pictures and stare. I mentioned I wanted to go into my room which was on the other side of the monastery and get them some brochures on Adoration.

They told me I had two minutes. I ran as fast as I could and grabbed a few of this and a few of that. I came back and met them outside.

UNITY FOR ALL

They let me film them with my cell phone. This was my first video of **A**nn and **T**erry from Connecticut, and they mentioned it was their first time in Adoration and they would come back with their family. I knew this was also His mission. I was to film chapels as much as I could with the free time that I had and evangelize. I promised God I would help in this way. I went back home and asked God to help me with a proper name for this website.

I went online and designed <u>Adoration Today.TV</u>. I forwarded everything to YouTube, and asked God to put souls in my path and Chapels and I would do all he asked of me.

Ann and Terry Outside of **Our Lady of Grace** Monastary, N. Guilford, CT.

I was so very grateful for the new job the Lord has given me since July 2016. I have five weeks vacation a year and this gives me time to do His will. The new website has helped me visit chapels in the USA, as well as speak as often as I feel inspired.

I met Father Peter Imaji, O.S.A., and was selected to lector when he does the Mass at the Sacred Heart in Lawrence on Tuesday evenings. This is a big step for me since I am shy of public speaking. Father Peter is here from Nigeria to receive his Masters in Education, and is an Augustinian Priest. He will go back to Nigeria in late June. He is now my Spiritual Director International. Father Peter has so many gifts and his time here was a blessing to many souls.

The mission continues and I know in God's time His will be done. As I look back at all the souls whose lives have changed and knowing how much they missed God, I have come to realize there is much work to do. On His time all things are possible.

God Bless!

Suzanne Mary DeCarolis
Founder of **Let The Light In Ministry**

www.letthelightinme.com
www.adorationtoday.tv
Email: suzdecarolis@comcast.net

TESTIMONIES

Steve Fleming story --- written by Steve Fleming

I am finally writing to you because I am once again moved spiritually by the thought of GOD's grace and mercy. I am filled with the holy spirit, but as usual, it is when my heart breaks that I am compelled to turn to GOD for blessings. I am not sure how to start this, but when Suzanne called for an appointment to discuss office supplies needs something told me that I should take the appointment to hear what she had to say. I didn't really need another office supply company and one that was working with was meeting my expectations. However, there was something....

Salespeople have a job to do and with all due respect, we usually thank each salesperson for stopping by but don't usually have a lot of time to discuss small savings that could potentially occur if the stars line up. Suzanne came into the office after a brief appointment made on the phone and was extremely organized and professional. It was humbling to me how well Suzanne was prepared for our meeting and her gentle but direct manner was appreciated. All the normal sales talk and then the sale was made. Not quite. Everything was much like described and we agreed to do business, but not until we shared a conversation about prayer and faith. The sale was made independent of our discussion about spirituality, but that part of it was the risky part. I am not sure who cast the first line, but we discussed spirituality and faith for at least 3 hours after we agreed to do business. During that time I learned of Suzanne struggle with a broken marriage of 23 years, and with a stutter. I also learned that Suzanne had turned to GOD because of these problems in her life. A friend of Suzanne's coworker had survived a serious illness and attributed his recovery to Suzanne prayers. I also believe that he recovered

UNITY FOR ALL

because of the power of prayer. Not long after meeting Suzanne, I had learned of a friend's sister who had a terminal cancerous brain tumor and young children. Like anyone who hears of a situation with little to no hope of recovery, it was upsetting. I then thought of Suzanne and asked her to pray for Jen. Although too unhealthy to immediately respond she eventually met Suzanne and attended church services. I believe it was a healing mass. Jen began to heal and her growing tumor slowed and then stopped growing and I believe it may have begun to shrink. I had passed this information on to Suzanne and Suzanne told me she had been praying for a complete recovery! I told this to Jen's sister and I know this was really great to hear. They also believe in the power of prayer.

I did not want to bother Suzanne, but there was one other friend, David, who suffered with a major heart attack while on a morning run. He was found on the sidewalk in the middle of his morning jogging route by construction workers and brought to the hospital. He was in a coma for a while and was having difficulty coming out of that coma. Things went from bad to worse and I thought, what would I do if anything happened to him and I did not ask Suzanne to include him in her prayers. Anyway, after the call for help went out for prayers, David began to improve to the point where he was out of his coma. It has been a long road back to health and he is still not there, but his turnaround coincided with a request for help.

Meeting Suzanne renewed a level of spirituality deep inside me that had been turned off by recent church events. I now pray the rosary almost daily and have become more GOD conscience on a daily basis.

UNITY FOR ALL

I have again taken shelter in GOD's love and my faith is strong again since meeting Suzanne. I believe in the power of prayer and I pray consistently, mostly for forgiveness, many times in thanks, and more occasionally for someone (including myself) in need of GOD's comfort, grace and mercy. I still have a way to go, but I believe in GOD and I believe in prayer, I thank GOD for my faith and I am thankful I had the opportunity to meet Suzanne.

Sincerely,

Steve Fleming, LSP, LEP

PRESIDENT-Vineyard Engineering & Environment Services, inc. – Stoneham, Mass.

I met Suzanne in March, 2014. We met at the Decolores Christian store in Salem, NH.

I planned on seeing a psychic but I found myself in this store for the first time. I arrived 15 min before closing. I started to walk around this store and asked the front desk a question. Suzanne was sitting on a table out front and the owner of the store asked if she could help me. I told them I was going to a psychic, but also looking for some angels.

Suzanne stood up and told me not to go to the psychic and if I heard of Adoration! I never heard of Adoration in my life. The store was closing and she told me a little about Adoration, and gave me her ministry card. She told me to find her on Facebook and she would explain more when I messaged her later.

I drove straight home and found her on Facebook. She sent me a link to her website, and asked me to read her story. I immediately called her and asked her if I could meet her at a chapel. I met Suzanne at Saint Mary's in Lawrence, Ma. We stayed for an hour. The peace was magnificent. I felt as if I belonged there and she told me my church had Adoration one day a week, and I should visit. I did. I took an hour consistently from 2014-2016. I now visit when I am able too.

Adoration is a big part of my life. My love for Jesus has grown considerably.

I have not gone to a psychic since and I do not plan to. Jesus has become my best friend and I encourage all seeking Peace to visit an Adoration Chapel.

Ann Marie Pellegrino

UNITY FOR ALL

Beth: Sept 2015

I met Suzanne at a workshop and told her about my sleeping disorder and Anxiety. She mentioned Adoration. I was originally Catholic but converted to Protestant in 2003. I had not been in a Catholic Church since becoming Protestant. I had been so wired and high anxiety it was approx 3 days of non sleeping, and weeks of not yawning. My body was exhausted and I could not sleep. I tried sleeping pills and nothing worked for me. I met her at Saint Joseph's in Wakefield, Mass. She told me to hold out my hands, as if to receive Jesus. She also held out her arms and we both prayed. I felt a peace within 5 minutes, and started yawning. I counted **33 YAWNS!** Suzanne looked at me and I was yawning non stop. I told her I was beginning to feel very tired after 20 minutes. I had to leave and drove home and went to bed. When I woke up the next day I had a wonderful peace that I never felt before. I believe Jesus helped me and took away the anxiety that had kept me awake for 3 days. Since this day I have been going to Adoration many more times and met Suzanne there. I have had many deep healings of other health issues. The doctors all know I am now spending my time in Adoration and are amazed at how good I am doing. I have since decided to become a Catholic again. My faith is stronger than it ever was in my life, and I owe it all to Adoration.

Adoration will continue to be a priority in my life. The peace is amazing.

Jesus, I trust in you!

Beth

UNITY FOR ALL

Caren: 2016

For those whom are constantly in pain I pray now with my whole heart and my soul that God the Father, Son and Holy Spirit help you to understand the depth of growing closer to my best friend through Adoration.

We lived in a small town when where we ran into someone I barely knew but knew her family from the past 40 years. We exchanged pleasantries, but there was something special about this Joyous woman that I was drawn too. Her face and her whole being were filled with Joy that I had not been close to in a lot of years. Yes, I was brought up Protestant, at the church of Open Bible, but I had gone to college in the South were I was babtized as a Born Again Christian. I had very special friendships with these when we are filled with God's Love and there was always someone to share with. For those whom are Blessed to have true friends whom follow the bible and struggle to live as GOD would want you know what I mean. He fills my life with good things so I stay young and strong like an Eagle. **Psalm 10.**

Spending time in Adoration with the Blessed Sacrament has changed my life considerably. I now seek Jesus in all things and his love is everlasting, as is His Peace. I find every time I am in front of the Blessed Sacrament I am filled with his Love, Peace and Joy.

If you are seeking answers go to an Adoration Chapel and surrender. You will be giving yourself back to God. Adoration is "Unity for All".

God Bless,

Caren

UNITY FOR ALL

Roseann Karlberg:

My name is Roseann Karlberg and I have lived in Tewksbury my whole life. I met Suzanne when I went to North Street School in first grade and went to her house when I was about seven years of age. We stayed in contact in High School and after about 15 years we connected again. She was always very hyper and active in her hobbies and her family. We have kept in touch by running into each other and would always get together. Many times we went out to dinner and talked about all the fun things we did in our earlier years.

In 2010, I went to her house and she spoke of Adoration. At that time I was Born Again and I never heard of it. She talked of this non stop and how her life had changed. I knew she was different because she was not talking quite as fast as she did when I remembered her. She had slowed down tremendously and had a sense of Peace. She invited my mother to her house and my mother knew immediately she felt an immediate peace. She talked of Adoration to my mother and my brother as well. I eventually met her at Adoration in Tewksbury. I have not been in a Catholic Church in over 40 years.

As I walked into this Chapel I Blessed myself with Holy water and bowed. I then proceeded to walk up to the altar and knelt down. I was there for about 10 minutes and not really understanding at that point what was to happen. I then sat in my chair to pray. I stayed for the hour and felt such peace. I knew why Suzanne enjoyed this and would go as often as I could.

It was 2011, and Suzanne was selling her house. She told me if I helped her stage it she would pay me and I needed the extra money. It was not an easy job and I worked during the day and she had much work to do.

We both worked together at night and we sometimes worked all night during the weekends. I remember we had to move these fence poles with concrete on them. I could not budge it from the ground or move it off the ground.

UNITY FOR ALL

I estimated them to weigh from 75 pounds and one at least 325 pounds. Suzanne said she could do it and she blessed herself first. I told her she could not do it and she had to hire someone. She blessed herself and picked one up as if it weighed nothing! I tried to move it and I could not move it at all. She moved all of them in sets of two and we relocated them. We took them to various places where they may need them. There was one left and I knew she could not do it because I could not do it. She was able to drag it and brought it to the back of her van. I told her together there was no way it would work. She insisted on the count of three and after she blessed herself that it would very easily go into the back of her van. I wanted to believe her but I did not know how I would get the strength to pick up the back end. On the count of three she did her end and I did mine and it didn't weigh much at all. I was in shock and she told me it was all GOD whom gave us the strength to move the biggest pole. She was not even tired and we moved it out of the yard. We had done all we had to do and it was days before she would be out of there. I knew because the house sold so fast we were also going to go to Fatima, Portugal in the coming months. There were strange things disappearing and then reappearing from her yard, like her Saint Joseph statue. She buried him upside down and could not find it. I helped her look for it but he was no where in the area she thought she put him. A few days before the closing he reappeared by the cherub statue. She picked him up and put him in a box. I also had been given permission to work there every day after work and wait for her to come home from work and we worked till midnight. It was a lot of fun while we worked together.

Her move happened and she was now living in an apartment in search of a house. I mentioned our trip to Fatima, Portugal one day and she was afraid to travel and I said, "but you promised". She agreed to take me and we made plans to travel. The flight was beautiful and peaceful. We stayed across the street from the Basilica. We went to Adoration every day and Mass. I remember being in Adoration which was under ground and it was very large in the chapel. We sat at least 50 feet away from the altar. I saw a boy's face the whole time I was there and I told Suzanne who said she did also. This was the first time I have seen a face in the Eucharist. I enjoyed this very much and it gave me a peace which increased my faith greatly. We met three people on November 11, 2011. They were ambassadors for the Blue Army International. Suzanne donated money to Veronica of the Figi Islands, who needed a statue of Mary for the Church in Africa. We took Veronica to the store in Portugal and Suzanne bought her a big statue to bring home. We visited many places while we were there. It was a very peaceful experience and one I will remember forever. I visited many places with Suzanne and I belong to many prayer groups with her. I began to realize I was not going to my own church anymore and I found a wonderful peace at Adoration. She invited me up to the Monastary in North Guilford, CT. I have gone here twice and stayed two weekends. One weekend with Suzanne and Luisa, I went into the chapel at midnight. They have Perpetual Adoration and I wanted to go alone without telling anyone. I was quite anxious and stressed out and thought this would be the best time to do it. I started speaking to Jesus from the altar. I did not know if the nuns were on the other side and thought I was alone. I had a lot on my mind and was seeking direction from Jesus.

I was beginning to feel frustrated and started talking louder and when this happened someone on the other side came into the Chapel. I then sat down and stared at the Eucharist and I saw His face. Jesus was staring at me for at least two hours. He was there and I was on the floor in a deep prayer. We stared and I knew He heard everything I had said to Him. I was totally convinced He was listening.

UNITY FOR ALL

The next day I told Suzanne about this and she was happy I was now receiving confirmation of His presence. I have now witnessed many things from Adoration. Jesus helped me sleep and gave me the peace I need in my life. I can go to Adoration and discuss anything and everything with Jesus. I feel a burden lift each time I leave the Chapel.

Suzanne kept asking me to come back and I was hesitant. I decided as time went by and after meeting Father Peter Imaji, from Nigeria it was time I come back to my Catholic Roots. I had spent eight years joining Suzanne in Adoration and several times to Mass. I enjoyed everything we did as friends and Catholic events. I found out I was babtized in 1961 at Saint Williams and received my first communion in 1971 at Saint Williams. All I had to do was go to confession and I did. I came back and I am forever to stay a Catholic.

I am forever blessed, changed, and grateful for learning about Adoration. I was hesitant at first, but I believe in time as your faith grows so does your love of all things. I would like to say if it were not for Suzanne I would have never known and would have never achieved such a Peace in my life.

God bless,
Roseann Karlberg
Apostle of Let the Light In Ministry

UNITY FOR ALL

Roseann Karlberg praying at St. Williams, Tewksbury, Ma.
Roseann became Catholic after 40 years away. The Blessed
Sacrament was her conversion back to Jesus.

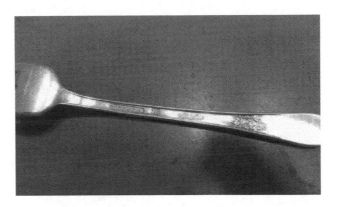

March - 2015----Silverware named "<u>ADORATION</u>".

I inherited this set of 8 from my Mother in 2015.

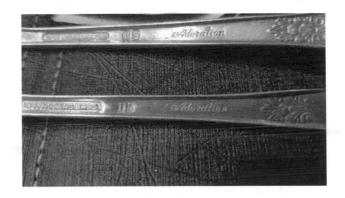

Lady Fatima - -0 5 1 2 – May 12, 2012.

UNITY FOR ALL

March 13th

UNITY FOR ALL

Adoration Chapel
St. Mary of the Assumption
Perpetual Adoration

Pauline DeCarolis sits on the bench
Donated by Suzanne M. DeCarolis in 2015
St. Mary of the Assumption- 300 Haverhill St.
Lawrence, Ma. 01840

UNITY FOR ALL

"The Greatest Gift You Can Give is The Gift of PEACE"

SAINT WILLIAMS OF YORK CATHOLIC CHURCH
1351 Main Street, Tewksbury, Ma. 01876
Perpetual Adoration

God Bless,
Suzanne M. DeCarolis

UNITY FOR ALL